TRANSFORMATION:
THE POETRY OF SPIRITUAL CONSCIOUSNESS

TRANSFORMATION:

THE POETRY OF SPIRITUAL CONSCIOUSNESS

Edited by Jay Ramsay

Rivelin Grapheme Press
in association with Egerton-Williams Studio
Hungerford & London

for Snowdon Barnett, its publisher

"The power of the word is a literal scientific fact. Through the operation of our thought forces we have creative power. The spoken word is nothing more or less than the outward expression of the workings of these interior forces. The spoken word is then, in a sense, the means whereby the thought forces are focused and directed along any particular line; and this concentration, this giving them direction, is necessary before any outward or material manifestation of their power can become evident."

– Ralph Waldo Trine, *In Tune with The Infinite*
first published by the Religious Book Club, 1897

Contents

Introduction (xi)

ON THE THRESHOLD (fire)

Seek Heart – Lemn Sissay 2

West Man – Alan Jackson 3
Poem For A Black South African – Barbara S. Cole 4
Orion – Bernard Saint 4
Human Mayflies – Carolyn Askar 5
Blind Angel – William Oxley 6
Shaman – Stephen Parr 7
Archbishop Romero – Bill Lewis 8
from TWA In Flight – Charles Lawrie 9
Illuminati – Bernard Saint 10
Chalcedon – Dinah Livingstone 11
Reconsidering – James Berry 13
The King – Shruti Pankaj 14
Beat It Out – John Agard 15
The Way Is Clear – Alan Jackson 15
Salamander – Bernard Saint 17
The Sibyl's Song – Michèle Roberts 17
My Refractory Heart – Gillian Allnutt 18
Love is Molten Gold-Path – Alan Rycroft 19
Michaelmas 1985 – Lanny Kennish 22

IN THE DARK (water)

Water Image – Gladys Mary Coles 26

The Tree – Andy Peters 27
In The Dark – Lizzie Spring 28
from Voices – Geoffrey Godbert 31
Dark – Georgina Lock 32
Hill – Moniza Alvi 32
Conjunctio – Timothy Atkins 33

The Heart – Paul Matthews 34
For The First Bird At Dawn – Harry Fainlight 34
Ending With A Line of Bronk's – Owen Davis 35
Anniversary – Lanny Kennish 36
For Sheila – Carol Fisher 37
Desolation – Libby Houston 37
from Skeleton Key – John Moat 38
Psyche And The Cat – Jo Loncelle 41
The Brick Kiln – Pippa Little 43
Showings – Anne Born 44
Winter Evening – May Ivimy 45
After The Darkness – Rosemary Palmeira 46

INTO ANOTHER WORLD (air)

"No water can vanish my fire" – Shruti Pankaj 50

Creation – Sara Jones 51
Writing A Poem – Raymond Tong 52
Symbols of Transformation – Desmond Tarrant 52
from Dossiers Secrets – Snowdon Barnett 53
from Tarot – Philip Kane 54
Nightmare – Les Tate 58
The Holy Fool – Rosemary Palmeira 59
Pilgrim Woman – Pippa Little 60
Rastaman – James Berry 62
The Spiritual – Bernard Saint 63
The Magic Coming Of Eclipse Dawns – Linda King 63
Behind The Cross – Shruti Pankaj 65
The Neverending Journey – Barbara S. Cole 66
from D'où Venons Nous? Que Sommes Nous? Où Allons Nous?
  – A.L. Hendriks 67
The Powers – Alan Jackson 71
The Lioness – Lizzie Spring 71
The Sounding Circle – Gladys Mary Coles 72
The Way – Andrea Clough 73
The Wheel – Rosemary Palmeira 73
Villa Di San Michele – Anne Born 74
Arriving Late At The End Of Time – Owen Davis 74
This Place – Sarah Peel 75

Excabbala – Harry Fainlight   76
There Were Three – Carolyn Askar   77
Into The Blaze Of Day – William Oxley   77
The Healer's Art – Alan Bleakley   78
Air – P.J. Kavanagh   79
The Poetry Of Birth – Geoffrey Godbert   80
Doubt Not That We Shall Found The City – Hilary Norman   81
What We Choose To See – Carolyn Askar   84
The Caravan – David Stuart Ryan   85
The Second Coming Over Lindisfarne – Charles Lawrie   86
New Age – Jay Ramsay   89
A Testament – Kathleen Raine   97

RESURRECTION & RETURN (earth)

Incarnation – Lanny Kennish   100

Return To Earth – Alan Rycroft   101
Aubade – Michael Horovitz   104
Morning – Stef Pixner   106
On Sighting The First Bluebell – Elaine Randell   107
Where Beauty Lies – Paul Matthews   107
Three Plants – Sara Boyes   108
The Party In The Woods – Peter Redgrove   110
Chrysalis – Penelope Shuttle   113
Time – Barbara Zanditon   114
Bringing The Geranium In For The Winter – Gillian Allnutt   116
Wolstonbury – Harry Fainlight   117
Elegy For Sally – Owen Davis   118
For All Who Fell In Wars Within And Without The Heart of Man
    – John Agard   120
Barlinnie: The World – Alan Jackson   122
Her Gift To Me – Michèle Roberts   124
Holomovement – Alan Bleakley   125
The Crossing Over – Pippa Little   127
Seal – P.J. Kavanagh   128
Second Look At A Cockroach – Heather Kirk   129
Things – Paul Matthews   129
Ordinary Things, Once Discovered Never Forgotten
    – Alan Bleakley   131

from Tantris – Stephen Parr   132
from Global Force – Taggart Deike   134
Paradise: A Regain - ? – Anna Taylor   136
The Hugging Child – John Horder   137
Gnome-flash – Charles Lawrie   137
When Children And Poets – Anna Taylor   138
First Visit To Glastonbury Tor – Annemarie Cooper   139
Joyful We Dance On The Tyrant Perfection – Barbara S. Cole   140
Touch – Bernard Saint   141
The Cross In the Milk – Bill Lewis   142
Stockwell Good Friday – Tony Lucas   142
Beyond All Other – Elaine Randell   144

* * * * *

The Witches Farmed Omens – Linda King   145
THE PITY OF THE WORLD – Lemn Sissay   145
The Angel And The Star – Lizzie Spring   145
Benediction – James Berry   146
"Tell them how easy love is" – *Elaine Randell*   146

Let The Centre Hold – Jehanne Mehta   147

Afterword   148

Acknowledgements   149

Brief Notes on Contributors   150

Frontispiece

The Mandala Drawing

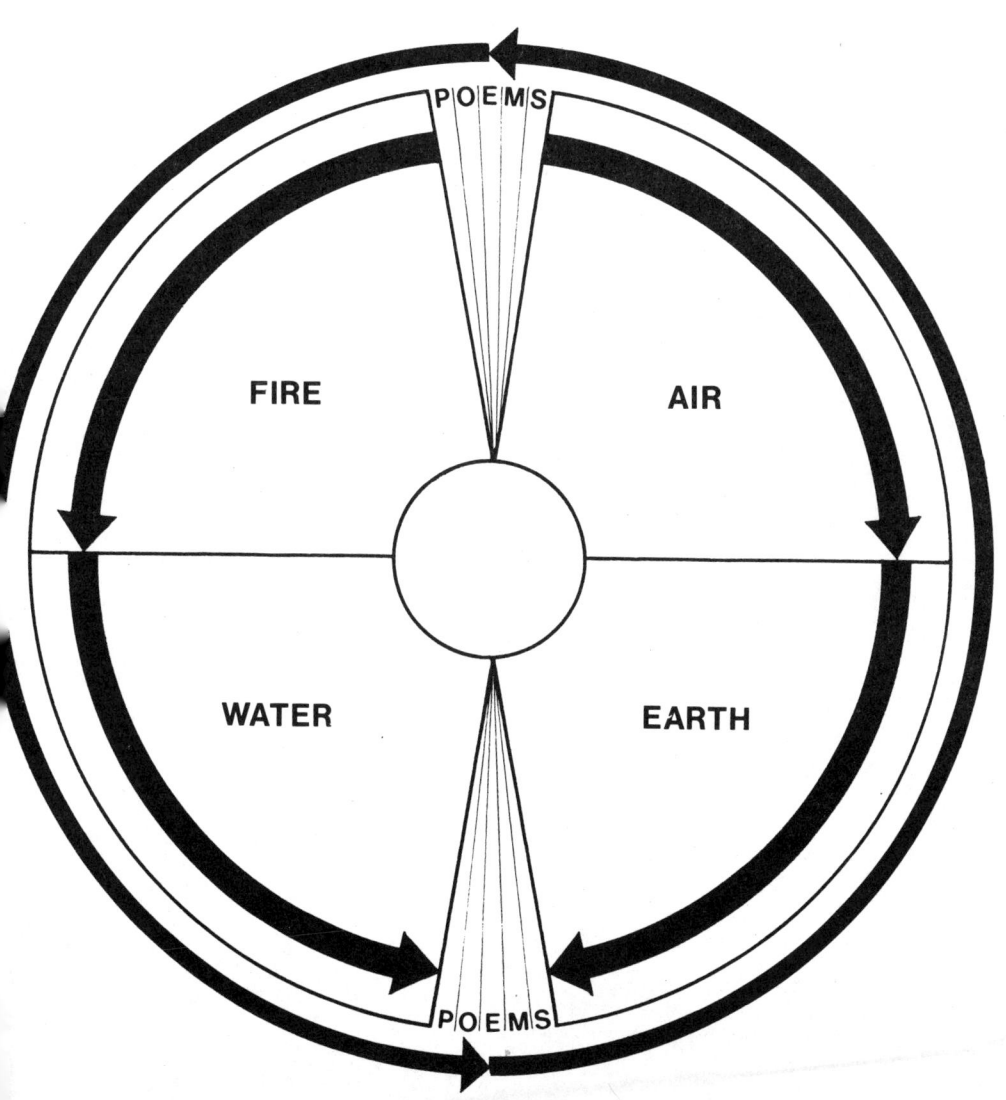

INTRODUCTION

This anthology brings together the work of a selection of contemporary poets living in Britain who represent what I believe is the front line: that is, transformation – a quality of change which day by day now is beginning to occur to us all as the prime value and purpose of our being here at this point in time. Much has been, and is being, published on this in related fields: but there is nothing of a collective nature that addresses this in the voices of those of us here now as poets, and in response to the question of what poetry has to do with it. That poetry has everything to do with it is not self-evident – I wish it was, and I'd rather be writing a poem that writing this.

Four years ago, out of exasperation with a literary scene that had little or nothing to do with what poetry is actually *for*, and out of a desire to affirm what it *is* for, I wrote a manifesto called *Psychic Poetry* which for me represented what was being left out of a discussion more preoccupied with personality and petty politics – in short, fashion rather than passion, reputation and shallow opportunism rather than the thing itself. At the same time, the work I was doing through Angels Of Fire (which culminated, at that stage, in the Chatto & Windus anthology I co-edited) was a concerted attempt by ourselves as a collective to offer in public an alternative for which we coined the term 'radical poetry' as a description of what was being both ignored and suppressed. The focus at that time was mainly political, because it needed to be: and the space Angels Of Fire created allowed a great deal that needed to be voiced to find its place and assert its commitment. My own experience was – to cut a long story short – that our major emphasis became our main limitation – a limitation which occurred to me in writing the manifesto, and which became increasingly obvious and unavoidable. What is essential to poetry was itself being avoided: what was really radical was being paid lip service to as an additional extra. The result was I began to see its shadow: a shadow made up of limited emotions in their own way just as reactionary and nihilistic as the status quo they were inspired to oppose. This is not to deny either what that anthology achieved, or that the issues themselves remain. What I am saying is that until those issues are grasped from inside, fully and not merely in theory, change itself is hypothetical.

I have said that those issues remain, and my choice of poems here also reflects them. The fact is we can change nothing until we change ourselves – and in changing ourselves, those issues also change. The problem comes through an attachment to what remains oppositional and is blocked from becoming transformational: anger and blame stagnate into self-righteousness, inverted egoism and revenge – and the shadow of power (whether collective or personal) in revealing its incapacity to love, devalues and disempowers itself. This is a complex and unresolved argument involving a fundamental need to bring politics and spirituality together in a synthesis that, at the time, Angels Of Fire was not capable of. Hence this anthology, at the root of which is personal change – its process and its alchemy. The nature of this lies at the essence of what this anthology proposes as poetic, through a poetry of spiritual values which are personally experienced, embodied and communicated as signals to the collective. That is to say we are where it begins – each of us, writers and readers alike. I would say further that the poet in all of us is what is most radical and most real, beyond the occupation of what literally being a poet entails.

Politics, as we know it, is at an impasse – the same impasse of materialism reached by economics ten years or so ago, and academic philosophy a decade before that. I had two things when I began editing this book – one was the symbol of the equal-armed Celtic cross (of 'resurrected life'), the other was a quotation from Jung written near the end of his life, prior to his dream of seeing great tracts of the planet devastated. He wrote: 'What our world lacks is the psychic connection, and no clique, no community of interests, no political party and no state will ever be able to replace this'. It is a sentiment echoed recently by Rudolf Bahro (one of the leading figures in the Green Movement in West Germany) in *Resurgence*. He puts it bluntly: 'The alternative movement is stagnating because it has no spiritual perspective', and asserts: 'Transformations can only come from the transformed'. We are part of a crisis of culture that politics is only capable of skimming the surface of with its crude oppositions and polarities, however necessary the emotions contained there have also been. We have realised that politics is personal – a vital realization essential to its renewal – but without work *on* the personal and all that that implies, this becomes a hollow credo: an excuse for taking things personally without actually taking responsibility (and a perpetuation, as often as not, of patriarchal energy). From a spiritual point of view, responsibility requires a further step, which is that we are all responsible for the world as it is and we all carry that world inside ourselves, whether we are conscious of it or not (the problem is that we are not). Here is the crisis, then, and the opportunity – and never so finely balanced as now. Another common fallacy is that we, personally, can do nothing. The fallacy conceals the reality: which is that the world, everywhere, exists between us, in relationship, and can do no more than reflect what our relationship to ourselves and those around us is. (Again the problem is no relationship.) The world is our mirror: and we can do nothing to change it by denying our own reflection. To see the world as it is, and where we are in it, means acknowledging its pain, and our own – the alternative is to deny that pain and project it on to others, the falsity of the projection belying our humanness. Likewise the evils of post-capitalism, technological heartlessness, racial and sexual discrimination and oppression – of everything that denies the poetic – are our own denial *en masse* of who we really are: that is our human tragedy, and it is a tragedy indivisible from the enormous process through which we are still learning what it is and means to be human. In a spiritual sense, transformation means all of us, having reached a point where it is no longer adequate to conceive of change as exclusive, as a limited privilege, as a 'luxury'. That is the most powerful of all the anti-spiritual conceptions that arise out of misdirected thinking: the spiritual is fundamental, and the story of our times is that we are being driven to recognise that for once and for all. Krishnamurti puts it briskly: 'Revolution, social, economic, can only change outer states and things, in increasing or narrowing circles, but it will always be within the limited field of thought. For total revolution the brain must forsake all its inward, secret mechanism of authority, envy, fear and so on'.

We need a politics that is psychologically mature, that refuses 'power over' (as Starhawk puts it) replacing it with 'power from within'. Personally we need to begin to withdraw our projections and in so doing recognise how through our own thoughts and imaginations we perpetuate the murderous unreality we are suffering and the breakdown it is causing – this dark before the dawn that can only be a dawn of our own choosing. It means a recognition of what it actually means to choose to be here, and choose life – which isn't as easy as we would like it to be. We need to see, in every sense, how this apocalypse of deathliness is serving us, and what it means to green the wasteland that is the devastated heart: our planet, and ourselves.

So what about our vision? our spirituality? This is, surely, the question, not least because of what separates us from it (and even, perhaps, from asking it). Transformation is as much about changes in spirituality and our notions of what it is – and everything I've said applies equally here. For many people, the whole concept of God, spirit, soul, faith and mystery is defined by negatives – not by experience, but by denial, and the limitations here are as overt. The problems are the same, fundamentally to do with power and its misuse that applies to the Church, its dogmatism and sectarianism, to gurus, leaders and organisations of all kinds in relationship to which radical spirituality has arisen. The New Age, whatever else it also is, is basically a vision of reclaiming and re-establishing us as beings of spirit, soul and body. It is a vision of affirmation and return to that vertical dimension through which we begin to live our birthright. Far from being a floating wishful idea, or an imposition of simplistic uniformity, its vision – in the truest sense of the word – is profoundly anarchic juxtaposed with earthly hierarchies, because its essence is re-empowerment. It is a vision, to use another phrase from Psychosynthesis, of 'what we may be' – and by implication already are (when we become willing to awaken to it). At the same time, in a non-orthodox sense, it is as profoundly religious – taking that word to its root, *religare*, which means to re-connect. It is not, as some people assume, a denial of the body, but an illumination of it from its source which is beyond the body – the same source from which we derive our actual beyond ego identity. It is metaphysical because we are metaphysical – we are souls living in time; and our lives are all journeys of the soul. In holistic terms it is the missing part without which the whole in any real sense is impossible to conceive of, let alone live. What so many of us have lost is what we are discovering, painfully and in confusion, that we cannot live without – we may go on surviving, absurdly believing that is all we are here for, or, more egoistically, denying both depth and height and claiming (in effect) the universe as a by-product of a Godless imagination – which is even more absurd. Or we may go further, which means beyond our intellect and its adolescence. Because change means, and must mean, change in consciousness and what we understand by consciousness – literally, of the way we 'see', through our limited five senses. Beyond them, we begin to touch on another world, and other levels of being available to an expanded awareness, and which in every way relate to our world here (in fact increasingly so the more we become aware of them). From a spiritual point of view, we are incarnate souls at different stages of personal evolution, and we each have access to a higher self that guides and oversees. Beyond our higher selves, the vastness of the spiritual world begins to open – both as our past and as our future, both individually and as a species. Our lives are inseparable from Creation itself. Again, spiritually speaking, we are innately creative and connected to every created thing – the light within us is within everything (as physicists have more recently recognised in quantum terms). Experienced beyond the mind with all its rationalisations and reductions, the implications of this are hard to find an adjective for. The revelation that we are not what we thought we were means that we can no longer see each other in the same way – or anything else, for that matter. The fantasy that we are mortal, isolated beings becomes increasingly difficult to sustain; and with that, the attitude which separates spiritual belief from what we begin to realise is also physical fact.

So what use is all this metaphysics? What does it mean? It means what we are here for, and what we are here to become: and that is spiritually human – neither one at the expense of the other, but both; which means re-owning both our divinity *and* our humanness, as a result of which our preconceptions about what either of those words tend to signify change (and with them, the language of their application). As spiritually human beings, as part of life, we are co-creators – we create reality. When we begin realizing this, and take responsibility for our creativity (or the lack of it) we can begin to change our reality – who we are, the way we live and talk, and what we wear and eat, the way we act – the way, if you like, we write our own lives on this page of air. The New Age movement, which comprises millions of us in every walk of life, is revolutionary because it is *e*volutionary: it is a movement dedicated to reconstruction, and to a healing that does not simply mean 'curing' (in a conventional medical sense), but means a suffering of meaning that is both an enlightening, and an opening of the heart to the wound of life and the darkness that is part of life: the 'loom of life', as Ruth White's discarnate guide Gildas points out, that we have all woven. By its nature, spiritual perception, in engaging what Gildas also calls 'the multifaceted jewel', reaches beyond polarization: everything is part of the pattern or process, in destruction and renewal, in dying and rebirth. Everything holds and embodies part of the truth: seen as it is, symbolically, in chaos and clarity. The dynamic centre of all this as it opens is what connects us to life – and that is the heart. The heart that connects us to life is also what enables us to channel our light *into* life – just as our minds channel ideas into form. The heart is transformation. This is why psychics speak of 'earthing the Light', of bringing it 'right down through' into our daily lives – and why inner work (whatever form it may take) is a protected space, a sacred space out of which each time we re-emerge into the world. That is the connection. As we begin to change, so we can change.

Our perceptions are widening. We are beginning to see each other as we are, and in the complexity of who we are. We are learning to include archetypal and spiritual energies not as 'fictions' but as an initiatory deepening of our identities beneath and above the existential personalities we name ourselves with. We are beginning to appreciate the context for the lives we are living, why we are living what we are living, and how that connects us karmically to the past. We are beginning to see the present for what it is: a preparation and a cleansing in which the old world is dying, and in which time, and our experience of time, is accelerating. We may even begin to envisage another dimension, not only on the other side of death, but here, where the future flows towards us, 'now'.

And we are unfinished. The New Age, with its tremendous vision and re-energization of the Christ spirit, is a working-out of many complex strands, methods, disciplines, and belief systems. I use the term as a popular (and also debased) reference: my interest in it is as idiosyncratic as my own influences, and with them, those experiences that have led me to understand what were at one time just words to me. Experience, and an openness to experience which includes the unknown, is the main thing – the mistake is in thinking we can get it all with our minds. At the same time, spiritual knowledge as a gathering force has itself shifted from the esoteric to the exoteric – it has come down, and there is less self-censorship in talking about it the more shared experience is made available. What was, until relatively recently, specialised and remote is no longer so. What we are witnessing, in fact, is a phenomenon, transcending the artificial boundaries of age division and the arrogance whereby one generation regards itself as superior to the previous one. The problem is that it's all too easy to get lost in it all – and here again, the yardstick has to be your own experience and inner authority (authority, that is, as opposed to 'reaction'). What is appropriate for one person to subscribe to is by no means necessarily the same as for another, any more than one person can tell another who God is. A religion of life is not only communal in the widest sense – it needs to be plural. Our lives, ultimately, are our paths. We are alone, and we are one another – and we are learning to realise why we need one another.

As George Trevelyan himself has written: 'The great transformation must begin in each one of us', and poetry is no exception. There is a vision, a process and a pilgrimage in these pages as a testimony, not only to the power and transparency of the medium, but also as a focusing towards the part poetry is playing – and the uniqueness of its contribution – in a wider context. Poetry has both held and prophesied this vision – and poets have imprisoned it in their own particular egotism. The poetry of transformation is a poetry of release – release and invocation, in which poets are also rediscovering what has been lost, in inspiration and in a very literal sense, 'vocation'. The poet who is conscious is a mediator, a transmitter, a witness and an exemplar – and in so far as poetry can be of service, it is something finally that calls to be lived; and first and foremost by the person who writes it. The American Indians call it 'walking your talk'. As a positive force, poetry and the experience of it is a magical catalyst; and its language, conceived as something not merely technical (though it is also that) is a manifestation of that unique voice we each have that is our real voice, the voice of your soul you access to become who you are, in the authenticity of your heart. When poetry becomes separated from that, like anything else, it becomes rather less than important; and if poetry has lost its vision in existential self-limitation and (dare I say it) trivialisation, it is also here to be reclaimed and redeemed. What else is it, after all, but a labour of love? and for love, and everything love can do.

The poetry scene is a microcosm of its kind. Some of the poets here are involved in all the on-going arguments, others are not and are not interested in being so. Some names here are known, others almost unknown beyond circles of friends: and it has been my intention to include as many lesser known names as I could, whose work so richly deserves to be read and heard. Everyone in this anthology, in their different ways, is aware of poetry as being something that has a form and is more than its form – and its purpose, by example, as being a realization of true personhood. For some here, poetry is primarily spiritual work, and its literary nature is directed and guided by that focus as its source. The poems themselves tell their own story.

This book is a journey. I have structured it as a mandala based on the energy of the four elements. Each individual poem (and poet) stands individually: and each form part of a whole that is a circle, and points towards the centre that is also that circle. It can be read like any other book in a linear way: at the same time, my feeling was that a new kind of anthology needed a new form allied to its context and contents. I want to say finally that for me the special pleasure in editing this was, and is, in realizing how many fellow travellers there are when I thought there were almost none. So many in fact, that I realised something new, something agelessly new, was being born. And there was only one word for that.

Jay Ramsay
February 1988

I
ON THE THRESHOLD
(fire)

Seek Heart

I see frozen ice
In listening eyes
In the back of their heads
I hear their cries

And heart beat thuds in me
For what i see
And heart beat thuds in me
For what i see

I see mist
Aching conceptions
And truth
Squandered in perceptions

And heart beat thuds in me
For what i see
And heart beat thuds in me
For what i see

Lemn Sissay

West Man

between gold and iron still hammered,
each living one of us,
keen to jingle and cleave,
in the west, that is, that I know of,
where the wind is red.

bearded in boats, they cut the ocean:
we singe air. The word's still: 'On'
which means To The End.

we cut the balls of god and killed his woman,
we'll take our freedom at all expense,
our eyes are screwed to telescopes,
our wind blows us off into space,
blows from a mouth
too wide to smile,
too deep for disobedience.

west man, maybe man, but I only say what I know,
is a killer, has hurt himself worst as must be,
and he stands now on the roof of the planet,
bare and pricked,
on an unleaved branch of a last tree,
listening to nothing,

                but the sound of himself,

thinking.

ALAN JACKSON

Poem For A Black South African

for Eugene Skeef

I hear your blood
scraping silent
sounds on the
history that
stands between
us like a
wall of broken
promises
and cries for
justice that
tumble down from
barren treetops
shaken by the
wind in early
morning
before the
flowers
are awake

BARBARA S. COLE

Orion

A northern town in winter,
Friday night closing time;
The bus station glares in a frost fire.
They see the longhair in his surplus parka
Waiting for the last bus out of here,
Carrying a Fender bass
In a soft case scrawled with band names,
An affirmation of his deities.

Knowing this they go for his fingers,
Kick him down to gravel,
Boot heels prise the hands, a stanley knife
Severs the tendons. No reason.

And the stars – they hold such clarity here
The milky way can be
Discerned as a trail of ash –
Look down from disdainful distance.

The stomping of the hapless boy
Pre-figured by ten years
The death of Victor Jarra,
Though this was neither for Orion's prize
Nor Jarra's revolution,

Its motives vague
As sin against the holy ghost,
And nearer human nature.

BERNARD SAINT

Human Mayflies

Mayflies
skim the surface,
skating
on water skin,
skirting lilies,
never settling.
Constant motion
prevents contact
with the heavy
element beneath.

Nectar-seeking,
they absorb nothing,
as they ricochet
from empty sweet
to sweet;
experiences
half-digested,
regurgitate
to dull the palate.

Watch them
flit on to
their potent
disillusionment.

CAROLYN ASKAR

Blind Angel

Not in sleep but awakening
the angel comes
lettered in the light of words
feathers burnished
more brilliant than autumn-varnished leaves
grass greener, shapes sharper
around his vivid figure
hands perfected by sculpture of prayer
eyes two concentrations
of seeing like fierce stars
labials that feed on love:
an everywhere-at-once figure
who stands in doorways
clouds of black light trailing
burning the quotidian moment
of domesticity and office
yet never crossing the threshold
of life, this minor existence
of ambition and avarice,

where the pale light of day
is not clear enough for him
nor really for anyone.

WILLIAM OXLEY

Shaman

for John Agard

Is this the way dawn
comes in your country –
a hushed leaning,
a breathing-out of
forgotten gods?

With your snake eyes
your hands flicking
like knotted lightning
you conjure
the single shy flower
out of our deserts

with your raven voice
your panther silence
you sing back
the green ghosts from childhood
that we have banished.

Poetry is a word for it.
we have not looked but
there is something new
in this room
walking with us –

soul, nakedness, our
severed knowledge.
Tonight, in Brixton
they are burning, maiming
looting for lack of it.

In Iran now
petrol bombs bloom orange
over ruins that were once
its oracle;
all our history has come down
to this:

Heart, without you
our world is narrower
and more lethal than
a knifepoint;
there must be no more shrinking.

going home beneath
icy stars, I pray:
snake, raven, panther
river of steep shadow
do not desert us

STEPHEN PARR

Archbishop Romero

once said in a speech
– the poor are Christ.
it was not long after
that the death squad
gunned him down as he
celebrated Mass. his

blood mixing with its
symbolic version on the
church floor in a
savage re-affirmation
of the sacrament.

somewhere, a factory wall
is spraycanned – Jesus Christ greatest LIVING revolutionary.
& down the dark
passage of history
on another wall a
graffiti fish swims
burning in its sea
of stone
pointing the WAYOUT
of a catacomb
into the light.

BILL LEWIS

from TWA In Flight (Series 2)

for Yoko

But how to make peace?

And the Anti-Christ shall come
Spread his black wing – as a raven
Fall like a forty-thousand-pound stone
On the hearts of the heroes of Russia;
Cold went the hearts of the heroes –
The darkness knew no degree; it was Death
No other, struggling for overlordship –
Earth-mastery, world-dominion,
welding all under the iron law –
sleek saloon, a bubble landscape, new moons;
flickering inner screens, endless inner television,
silent eerie electronic music,
stairs of glistening nylon,
sea-worms, weaving to the stars,
all earth a bread-pellet, artificial proteins –
Nourishless the life and soul of men
dulls in a spirit mechanism –
Dull dark absolute machine –
I say you have no strength to stand

the Word of God
through whom I move,
says Christ in me,
even the hardest stone
earth's barren coin
to

        love, love, love –

CHARLES LAWRIE

Illuminati

Because we believed
The first love, not the last
Adhered to in exhaustion with no choice

We founded the shopping cathedral
With every symbol but the cross.

We founded the cathedral
We worshipped her catalogue
We advanced in the pride of comparison

And we founded the vertical publishing house
With no exit and no heart.

We founded the autocephallic library
As relief from meaningless work
And the fruits of our minds divided us.

We founded the universal factory
Which feeds, clothes, and saves,
In which all become redundant

And we entered the computer age
And the age of alienation
And the last days

While the child inside
Dreamt of dolphins rising
Through the sea of the kingdom of healing

Whose world this is going to be.
If we are going to be.

BERNARD SAINT

Chalcedon

Not the gnosis of an elect
self-selected elite
calling their slight trendy insights
an exclusive enlightenment.
The principal part of speech is verb
and the word saves in time, becomes flesh,
submits to passion, shines in resurrection.
It speaks to all, of all, for all,
it connects, it expresses the people.
Great or small it says how things are,
tells the truth strongly and sweetly.
It names wrongs, rages, castigates,
soothsays, praises, prophesies,
propounds possible harmonies,
earthly heavens, happy days.

It must do it well,
expertly, be superb;
it is not fluid conversation.
It is conceived alone
and when it arrives to be enrolled,
may be unwelcome, no room for it.
Pains have to be suffered at its coming,
which is hard labour, uncomfortable.
It must cost, strive for perfection
and then stop at that.

And one and the same body of words,
piece of work, doing poem,
one subsistence, one hypostasis,
one voice, one face,
whose effect, like its existence,
is not all in the clouds,
no mere object of contemplation,
but which speaks on a historical occasion
(then again) and when it works,
the power of its sound burns:

has not a single nature, *physis*,
it has two;
and is apprehended in two ways.
When we are gathered together
and it is uttered we hear it,
and when I want to be quiet I read.
The latter as print, text in view,
though it is notation
of the noise of the other,
is yet a distinct nature,
unconfused, and the difference
in no way diminished because of the union
of one and the same subsistence
– word incarnate –
in two natures distinct not separate.

So let us celebrate
not cool detachment of the business spirit,
not the enrichment of a clique,
not gnosis of fashionable hierarchies,
not initiation into dominations, thrones,
to kick competitors and scale to the top quick,
not pseudo-enlightenment of name-dropping and cheap puns,
not spite, logic-chopping, profiteering,
not the appropriation of the word hoard,
or the privatisation of any public treasure.

But in two natures one poem,
redeeming word, wisdom,
pouring itself out,
coming down,
kenosis, katabasis, harrowing of hell,
taking it all on,
to embody, suffer, transform,
the whole, for the life of it,
for the healing
of the whole people.

DINAH LIVINGSTONE

Note
The Council of Chalcedon in 451 defined the saving incarnate word as one subsistence of two natures. Greek terms in the poem: *physis:* nature; *kenosis:* emptying; *katabasis:* going down.

Reconsidering

Afterwards
the argument impressed me much.

I saw we suspect all life is good
and it is response
that makes it otherwise.
So to dispel any truth in that
we cajole each other to hypocrites.

Hardest of all is how
not to be a hypocrite.
Everybody cajoles everybody
to be a hypocrite.

And especially
a chosen leader must first show
being the most adept at it.

JAMES BERRY

The King

Only a child can proclaim,
Oh! The King has no clothes –

Only a youth can declare,
Why the King! And what Kingdom?

Only the aged will agree,
The King can do no wrong –

Only the philosophers could maintain:
I hate the King, but I love the man –

Only a prophet could preach,
The kingdom of heaven is not for
The kings of the earth –

Only a poet can sing,
One who rules the heart is a slave,
One who is ruled is a king —

SHRUTI PANKAJ

Beat It Out

Beat it out man
beat out the hurt
beat it out
to riddum of steel/
feel
panblood flow
watch the dream
grow
from things unshaped
to real/
beat it out man
beat it out
beat out the rape
of the whip
shadow
the burn and blow
on gaping skin/
beat it out man
beat it out
beat out the weight
of history
scar/and/hate

beat it out man
beat it out
beat out the bleed
and spill
of seed
to waste/
beat it out man
beat it out
beat out
a new message
from de middle/
passage
womb of riddle/
beat it out man
beat it out
beat out the burden
of history
sound
beat it/heal it/shape it
confound
wounds
with vision

JOHN AGARD

The Way Is Clear

The world's being brought to oneness under the power of death

    And yet the way is clear

The limited mental consciousness crumbles daily under the impact of evil

    And yet the way is clear

The media, machinery and fantasy-fashion-products enslave millions of minds

        And yet the way is clear

Mechanistic legalistic materialist political and scientific concepts prevent understanding of humanity as a being among beings

        And yet the way is clear

Old gods, and worse than old gods, are being revived because persons will not suffer the struggle of good and evil in their hearts

        And yet the way is clear

The world moves visibly towards titanic disaster whether of fire or suffocation

        And yet the way is clear

The rabbis priests and ministers still haunt their melancholy erections

        And yet the way is clear

The artists take their gifts for granted and do not acknowledge the angels they unconsciously receive from

        And yet the way is clear

The ritualists and fundamentalists revive their empty forms and are inevitably compelled to legislate and kill

        And yet the way is clear

The masses define their meaning in relation to the work-machine which is like manacling yourself to a skeleton

        And yet

the lonely investigating spirits of the brothers and sisters who acknowledge love as their goal and so consciously take up their destiny will not be defeated; and, through great reaches of time, the earth, yes, will comes to its fulfilment resolution and transformation, for I have seen that, in the mind of time

        And the way is clear

ALAN JACKSON

Salamander

Your long dark-gold tongue
Ignites the earth's entrance,

Leaves this well medicinal, and you?
Vulnerable invincible as mercury.

Blood insists continuum; and shed and re-assume
The fire-coat the singing pattern.

A witness without status in this world,
Prophet immersed and rising

Where the clear pool breaks to heal
Endless effortless spirit.

Ancient king, reviled, unrobed,
You bring improbable fire:

Bush that springs to move in the desert,
Affirmation, sex, and resurrection.

                                        BERNARD SAINT

The Sibyl's Song

having hooded my face with hair
having hung, all night long
lips apart, over a silent pit

having crouched, having borne down
and down, having yelled
having delivered myself

having danced, having bitten
cloth, beaten air
until the song came

having delivered myself of a strong song
I collapse, gasping, with dissolved bones

she who came to me, she who called out loud
she who licked at my ear
like flame, and sank in
deep as a wound, she who swelled in me

she whose winged breath
wrestles with mud and
shapes it to pots and houses
she is my lady, she is the secret word

having lain with many men
having remained virgin: unmarried
having loved women, having shown
forth my big belly, my songs

I shall burn for this

I will sing high in the fire
oh let the fierce goddess come

MICHÈLE ROBERTS

My Refractory Heart

too hot little heart   untouchable
you burned your way out of the cradle like a bald fireball

you're burning a hole in my nightdress
it's inflammable

you're burning a hole in my chest   like a red apple sun
bursting out of the mist

you're turning me into a statue of the most blest
virgin   in the corridor of my first school   God

wouldn't let a sparrow fall   you know   but I forget
God doesn't yet exist   God made my soul   but

you were begotten of   in the beginning the bough did
break   the cradle fall   and you were

not a windfall or a lark   a little sunbeam   but a star
lost in the everlasting

hour of dark December night wherein the moon sails not
to save me   I am

out of the frying pan here   my little fish
on fire

I rock you in the cradle of my ear   I wrap you
in my hair   and everywhere   the ghost of my old mother

fear   dissolves like love in a mist   I've lit the gas
fire   why belittle you   now

hear my word for you   dear heart   dear all things great and small and
irrefrangible   yes   you deserve that

GILLIAN ALLNUTT

Love Is Molten Gold-Path

Love, is molten gold-path
infernoed roses pyre the sky
a fire-walk on the freeways of the sea
scintillating white and brilliant
a splendour still and floating
the unfurling new
now
alchemy
of every living
dying
I-wave
weaving the heaved marvel of inconstancy
the blue, bled robes of our sea.

Will you go now?
take my hand;
it's burning
walk the long bleed of the waters
torch jettisoned to heart
dare to ignite again
the flowering inferno
fuse of wound,
the fire flares
tender
in the sparkless tinders of our longing,
the frigid candle of your body
opens
the wax of too set selves melting
in the pain
to burgeon the conflagration
of your ecstasy.

We have loved
where love is not
only the lash and smile of a rose
that hides a welter of thorns
for everyone turns
from the heart's unturning light –
shades it, lauds it,
mauls and maws it,
contracts
manipulates
abuses, it.
The heart is reached for
through a thousand minds and bodies
but it is not touched;
but still we reach, desperate
through the rend of dark
for the impossible palm
that holds us to the fire's firm;
for to retract the hand
is the only withering
the rose, irrepressible petals of the heart's perennials
can ever know.

Will you be, courageously?
and walk across your waters
where you're lamed
though you see no other dancer
mount your molten threshold yet;
you've sunk so many times before
to see the loam and shipwreck
of your load of loves beneath you;
their cries of sunken cargoes
the weight and haunt of tears
that tear you with the broken years
and ceaseless shiftings of the sand
long as you thrust through wound of waves
and live the love of man.

Withholding all commitment
we dally and daze from doll to doll till death –
money, knowledge, power, lust
animals, children, churches;
all idols that we cling to
for want of the fire of real
in man or woman.
Surely, we have never been
so apart as now.
The call of the clear heart
whose cry sears to the bone
of the brokenness that heals
must attract in the end
a heart that resonates
to its seal of trust,
to golden on the waters
as together.
And whether we're given
three months or thirty years
death rots
and separation stalks so stealthily
all we would embrace
but still, and this is the white-hot searing of us all
we must reach out for fire
through the tindering and the fuel of forms that pass
to find us
in the lost eternities of the heart.

ALAN RYCROFT

Michaelmas 1985

Shall we come to You
in freedom, or in fear?

Because we love You,
or we shiver at our fate?

The guardians of the Mysteries
are merciful,

But they are generous
if we work.

I write with the swift ink
of cataracts,

Impetuous to tell
what I have seen:

The dragon grinning,
coiled around the world;

In his dry grip
he holds it tight.

But say his name
and his great claws retract,

Say his name, and
his rough heart is faint.

Pray for the man
whom the dragon has swallowed;

Pray for him, and
the dragon will spew him out.

And I have seen the fire
at the centre of the ring,

The white hair of the priests
in the luminous night.

They have given their life,
they have given their sinew,

They have given their love
to the ineffable fire.

One day we will speak like fire,
the way You do;

The rest is all profanity.

LANNY KENNISH

FIRE   AIR

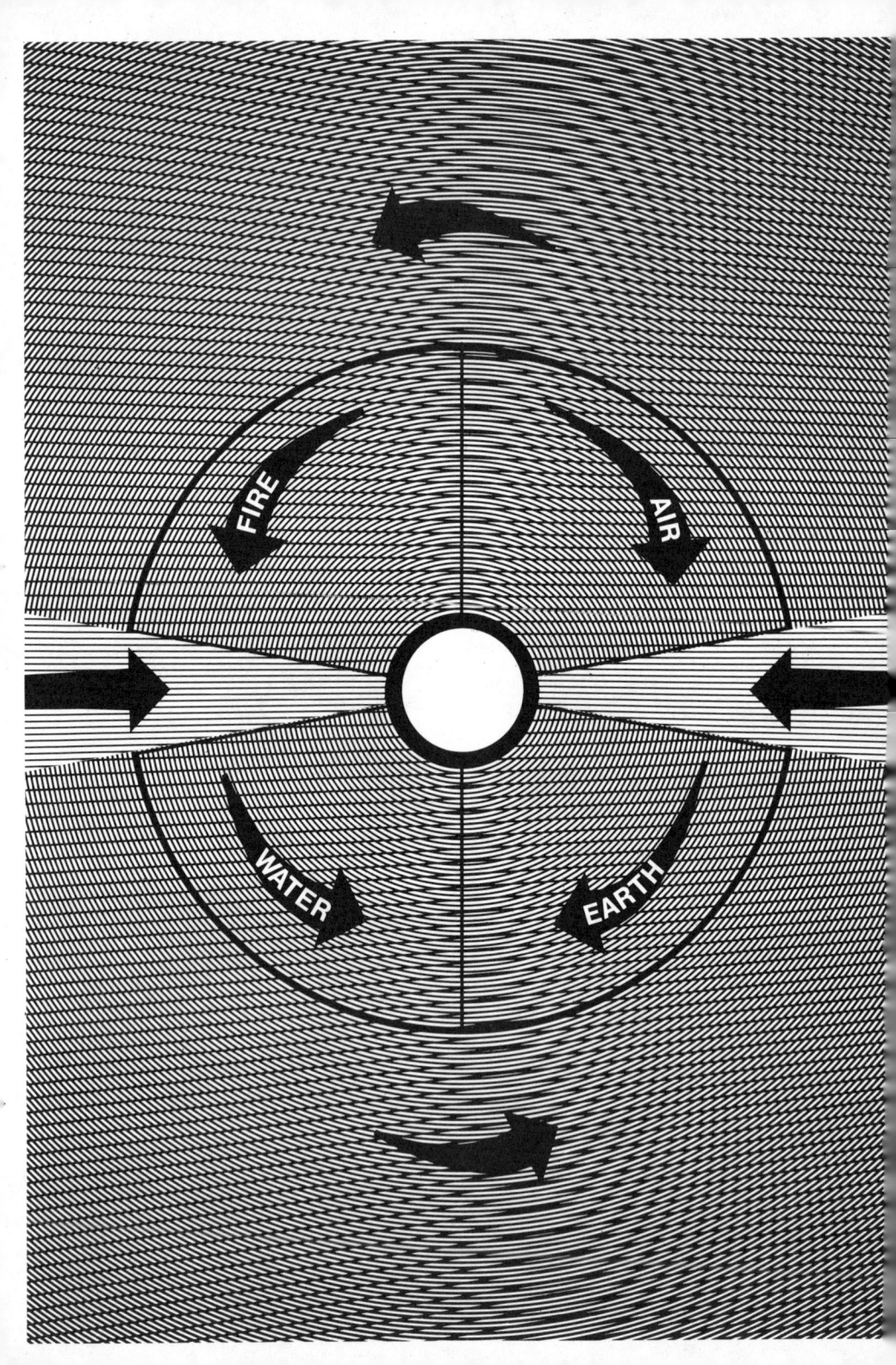

WATER   EARTH

II

IN THE DARK

(water)

Water Image

Raindrops drip from the lime trees
laburnum chandeliers are citrus wet
the last shrinking blossom on the hawthorn
drowns in resignation to forget
and the new golden rose is liquid yet.

Gladys Mary Coles

The Tree

You pierce my hands
and I am dying;
I cry with tears of blood
the nails piercing
and oh! it hurts so much.
This blood of my passion stains the wood;
it pains me.
I am spent now, my blood splashing down,
tears of passionate falling
and I am dying.
The Tree sinks into the ground, oily and filthy with
pain
and trodden.
The Tree is falling now.
The sun is sinking, my lips dry as stone;
my cry dies into the ground, no sound

And the fallen seeds, calling out,
deep, dark (buried inside with stone),
aching like the mountain, a city
to be soft, soaked, loved by Love.
And the seeds are wet with tears of blood,
washed now, wild with passion;
seeds of Love dancing like a mountain.

Pluck out the nails of poison in my land!
My hands and arms are pierced and I am hurting.
Pluck out! Pluck. Pluck out
the nails of poison, like a city, a mountain.

But the seeds, deep, darkasblood,
stonesfalling, mountains heavyspent;
it pains me.
Yes we are wild with the trodden sun
and passion plucked out,
poisoned like a city with tears of stone,
I am alone.

Love sinks into the ground,
no sound.
Love, piercing, untrodden, calling out,
so heavy now.
Sun plucked out and the soft
blood in my hands full of stone,

And I taste the salty nails that pierce
like cities,
and the tree
the tree, is falling like a stone

it pains me
it pains me
oh it pains me

ANDY PETERS

In The Dark 1

Night time,
in the dark,
in the winter
in darkness longer than light.

Calling for heavenly fire
receiving glimmers of hellfire
which consumes all that falls in its maw,
burning,
burning
in the tangible breath
of midnight.

Help me to stay safe.
I do not desire to fall
tonight,
this night,
now.

But, as I dream,
I wander.
Simply in the closing of my eyes,
I see myself slip sideways,
so easy to channel,
    to funnel
into that fiery pit.

Oh, lighten my darkness,
I beseech you;
but not with burning,
I beg of you:
my wings scorch easily
and I should like to dance for you,
dance with grace and delicacy,
such fleetness flying over that yawning gap,
such art and beauty all for you.

But, where are you?
Hidden among the moving shadows?
Gone down the blind years?
Consumed in your own light?
Oh, where are you?

It is night time,
in the dark,
and in the winter
we are in darkness
much longer than
in that thin light of day.

In The Dark 2

It is necessary
to do that which
the inner journey dictates.
To do otherwise
is to fly
into all the faces of adversity
towards certain death
without choice of transformation.
It is necessary to submit.
These creasing aching breaking
pressures
will force one
out of the   old skin
             old bones
             old body
the old pattern pulverised.
So, conceive of choosing to move,
to travel a little further
into what one may become:
a new growth.
A splitting spurting self
which cannot be achieved
without that destruction of the old,
the dereliction and relinquishing
of the previous.

Oh yes, pain is often experienced
during critical phases.
And so, I am gone into the dark places of noon
and there is a chill upon me.
I hear no one,
nothing but the scuffle of leaves
over the face of the earth.
Are you to be found,
any more than the hope of a glimmer of a candle
in the depths of this cavern?
Then, if you are,
let me ask this, this
as many a man before me:

How long, oh lord, how long?
For, let it not be forgotten
that still I should like to dance for you,
dance with such grace and delicacy
across that yawning gap
with such fleetness,
let it be remembered:
still do I wish to dance for you.

LIZZIE SPRING

from Voices

12

i have therefore shed my skin.
i bleed, bruise easily.
i cannot always breathe.
a sword is being pulled out of me.
i am pacified by hands.
when i sleep i always dream.
when i waken i always remember.
i am reaching the other side.
i have passed through all religions.
i no longer need any work.
there are very few words
i have to listen for.
i have messages from the world.
voices are always with me.
the comfort i feel is a light.
the comfort i feel is a light
which has been in darkness.
i have therefore shed my skin.
(i bleed, bruise easily.
i cannot always breathe.
a sword is being pulled out of me).

GEOFFREY GODBERT

Dark

I'm creeping slowly into dark.
Which questions should I take to ask
the little girl within?

Each division seems unreal.
Each 'What do I believe?' irrelevant
to the wordless knowledge clinging
to the crook of my spine.

Past and future cave in instants.
I'm here now, living night quietly.
Prithee lie thee down beside me.
Dream of peace.

GEORGINA LOCK

Hill

The hill heaps up her darknesses.

It is too cold for me to reach
the top, yet she is always supreme,

dropping the lakes to her feet
and brushing them with her full skirt.

She'll never stoop down to her domain
now she has the luxury of a view.

In charge of greys and green-greys
she structures the late afternoon

with inky threads from stalling kites
and the hurtlings of solo footballers.

Slowly, she discards all detail –
offers me her dissolving horizons.

MONIZA ALVI

Conjunctio

In the belly
The bass voice
Is open & still
The eyes need
No mark. The
Candles are low
And the river
Is full. The
Night is a road
I am lost on
Beneath a full
Circle
All our maps
Must be white

Beneath your
Parting moon
Hold this shadow
It is warm
From this heat
What we share
Leads a core
Of all hours
The small coin
Of self sparkles
And slips

At high water
Glittering light
And fish
Fill the sound
The basket to
Hold us
We weave
From the night

TIMOTHY ATKINS

The Heart

Coming to write this
I am lonely. I am lost. My heart
is alone here in the act.

Wife asleep. Children asleep.
Struggling to write this.

My heart bangs wildly. Midnight.
When everything. When the heart
threatens to become a window.

And what's on the other side?

The poem is. It moves there.
It moves the heart.

To receive the poem it is required
that we abandon poetry.

PAUL MATTHEWS

For The First Bird At Dawn

Sing on, unpublished one, O unpolluted throat,
Delicately broaching those depths that silently

Gathered nightlong, filling, brimming;
Released now in these pure, deliberately upwelling notes.

Heartspring that, nightlong,
thought through accumulated thought drilled, rasping;

My throat parching for its voice as I stumbled,
Toiling through the mind's blackness, across the blinding page.

HARRY FAINLIGHT

Ending With A Line Of Bronk's

for Adam

Grained air gnaws the castle's bones.
I find sharp pleasure in solitude,
Walking hill down to heath and harbour.

Far off, between the breathing reeds
And the crabclaw-scented islands,
A brotherhood of sea-birds jostles over the ceiling tide,

Sending faint sobs to the heart of the poem.
The sea preys on its own debris, as I do on mine.
The hours that mark out what's given to a larger remembering

From what merely must be dealt with and disposed of,
I count them, as if counting deaths, that whilst never
Killing me, reduce and reduce my heart

Till it and dust could not be separated,
Till I am left to step along with beauty as a kind of beast.
I wane while all else waxes, or seems to –

For it is springtime. The upturned cups of daffodils
Spill out a yellow stain. I cannot flee the absolute,
And I cannot say I seek it out. Though I wish I could.

But it watches me, I know that. Watches over me.
And it stands close – I know that, too.
The rain-clouds' edges are burnished with late shafts of sun:

One of the signs I'm guarded, who wastes away
His given graces saying that he's sad for lack of them.
Under my feet, shafts of a dripping darkness

Quarry more darkness, and more – more than a night could hold.
Even there, that deep, a light, though black, is shining.
Salt, little son, spells sea, and tears, and the labour

Living calls us to. And then death calls.
All my poems caress that word, I dread its sweet repose less
Because I know these hills and heathers speak me

More clearly than I could ever speak myself.
As we walk, I teach you names, Adam, knowing each new name you learn
Will nail up the nameless in a coffin of words.

Inevitable sanctity my only excuse.
We are spared because of it.
The clarity that words can make is not about the world.

OWEN DAVIS

Anniversary

July 18, 1974

Nothing keeps so well
As a creel of memories
Angled from the main chance:

On a bright day in Dublin
By the Bay,
Idling on the sun-blind sand;

On a black day while the Atlantic
Pursues a furious flirtation
With the north rock of Tiree.

Youth is a basket of succulent fish
In flashy excess of the quota;

We have exchanged our young gifts
Without pause, and now,
At the ebb-flow of young blood,
Love glides deeper
Than the deep sea-bed,
Luminous beyond the hook of death.

LANNY KENNISH

For Sheila

These October trees!
Gazed at through glass,
They burn unconsumed;
Received direct in the open air
Flamethrowers searing the vision;
All glancing is edged with fire.

And you in a bar
Passionately talk,
Your drink unconsumed,
Of trees and roots: an incandescence
Derived, you remind us, from what
Darkspreading, underearth strengths!

CAROL FISHER

Desolution

blue as ice   but not cold   no
sea green   but not wet   this
deep abyss   bright   bright as mist

my whole past flashed past last
time I surfaced guess it's still
up there careering about

or   lifeless raft   rocked bland
sits like some dumb microland
gulls use   let them   I float down

look   it does not drown

LIBBY HOUSTON

from Skeleton Key

*I sing this autumn
after mid-summer's dying, before I turn cold
to mid-winter's desolate wisdom.*

*I may not write verse better than this. September
is colours of the earth, is beaten gold.
Sunlight conceals the patina.*

*For me all that is certain
is in shadow. She is alive – in the gold,
in the harvest, in the torch-light procession.*

2

"Never! I'd sooner
Death to sleep with me." *Sleep with me.*
I am drawn to the water.

The ripple is still. Only the echo rings.
"… Come to me." *Come to me.*
This child can sing.

It's my name he whispers:
"… lie with me." *Die with me.*
He lifts his lips. Breath clouds the water.

6

A cry in the mist – *The dolphin squeal.*
Curlew shrill in the storm.
The whole deep-belling whale.

*Cow yawn, cabbage, the screech of grass,
the spider's. The worm's
or the woman's.* All joyous,

no more dragged out. The whipped scud congeals
in the bowl, forms
the one word, the wine in the grail.

10

Her sleep is monstrous.
Her smile is the moon set on her lips.
And I'm reduced to a swine's husk.

A god grunt and tremble? She took me for a man.
Caught in that grip
I was everything.

Now without lust
I am nothing – she has stripped
me to the light. I turn on her disgust.

23

Breathless her lips. Now the night's noon
and the sound of the stream
out loud fall about our room.

She dead asleep, while I feel night
come wondering between
us – and steel her to the light.

Lids flicker before the dawn:
wings rippling the dream's
glass. She looks about her, and is born.

28

Her name escapes me; the leaves,
there yesterday, are fallen. Frost –
and the winter beast breathes

slow to not mist the glass,
the last sound is lost,
held beyond thought in the third eye of ice;

and coldly he sees
a girl, not a ghost,
come bodily from the shade to bind the sheaves.

32

After rain
the valley will brim with birdsong.
In the orchard the mole is digging again,

his hill mountains. Water
envelopes the earth. I have longed
for a child – can hear his laughter

down by the tense stream –
and nearby her clear voice, against the storm
and the gull's distant scream.

34

Turned back at Gull Rock
by the sea's silent drift,
warned away by the bones of ghosts, the croak

and cruel warning eye of the mother bird
white-wheeling under the cliff –
there overhead

caught the cloud's eye, the window of a shack
where still and cold as death
the poet takes stock.

Breath is ceremony, is leaf to the bole;
but life unpolished
is unbearable – until a stone bring up the burnish.

As if a vizor of gold must shield the eyes
from so much violence. But are you meanwhile
alive? You have aged. But not your eyes.

I see nothing diminish.
I imagine your smile.
You are alive in the gold, and gold will not tarnish.

JOHN MOAT

Psyche And The Cat

for Jocken Encke

She knew he had a great respect for the way
she delved within her fragile soul
with the tenacity of the Goat
under which she was born

He knew she respected him for the quiet
presence with which he stayed with her
despite her wanting to be totally immersed
in him, penetrated by him and made significant by him

She had had the courage to remain in
unknown territory for long periods of time
like her sister Ereshkigal in the underworld
she fought many daimons and as a reward
was stripped and impaled
on the pole of despair and meaninglessness

She had shared more than the loneliness
and unheld feelings of her childhood
she had also shared her future
and the pain of her present
while he gently pointed her
unhurriedly towards her center

Before or shortly before her descent
she had found a cat or rather
a cat had found her
in her fantasy
the cat was often sitting on her lap
it protected her in her wanderings
and reminded her of
the sacred nature of the task

At times, she behaved like a cat
about to kill her own offspring
in the face of danger
particularly when pleasure and joy
threatened to overcome her life

She was so used to the dark
she'd always lived with the dark
and like the cat
she could even see better in the dark

He had to tame her slowly time after time
and indicate the light with circumspection
in case she would retreat
to the blackness if threatened
by the prospect of hope

After a few minutes of silence
in which she adjusted
from the outside to the inside
she used to say: I had a dream

She always wanted him
to hold and address the dreams
because she couldn't encompass them
and they overwhelmed her
but she soon realized
they didn't entirely belong to her

Later and rather tentatively at first
she started daring the dreams
to live in her and guide her
she learnt a new kind of humility
she was the dreams but the dreams weren't hers

One day, he shook hands with her
but this time the touch felt different
partly because he took her hand with both of his

There was so much acknowledgement in the gesture
as if to thank her for her unrelenting attempt
at inhabiting herself and at sharing it with him

Now he could grant her freely his protection
because she had developed her own from within

Yet the war was a serious threat in the Gulf
and her lover was about to go again

But now she dreamt of mansions
with warm timber on the facades

There was hope to withstand the cracks

JO LONCELLE

The Brick Kiln

for Frida Kahlo

You, who came here at the end
(night is falling in my life)
saw the oven work its leathery smoke,
shards crackling underfoot and the few, hard leaves
scratching like fingernails
on the walls and roads;
you saw your death-place here,
in the brick kiln thick as your mother's waist.
You knew it would come, this
curious, numb hush
of leafless grays and browns,
sediment of passions –
you took the brush in your hands,
allowed death to happen.

But first you wound your bloodline,
that tough artery needy and defiant
as your monkey-babies, strapped it
hard across your body
so it embraced your jagged spine,
cradled your heart (angry as a fist)
and twisted in your hair,
still hungry –
so that when, afterwards, they brought you here
you were incendiary, the oil and tears
in your hair flared, caught fire,
the last ring on your finger melted,
cracked open.
You, who birthed yourself
with both hands all your life,
haul on the mother-vine, snaky
blood-rich umbilicus;
once more, sleep awhile
here at white heat.
Impervious the old skin burns,
another birth begins.

PIPPA LITTLE

Showings

One of those clouded days when blue comes through
as grey. Long winter, dark.
Walking, sorrow's blindfold
covered sight, ears dulled
with silence deaf to the waves.
Driving, stuck to old routes, thoughts like glue.

The moorspine, humped above greygreen fields
came into view. Then its line
grew clear: blue restated blue.
And that return of colour freed sight,
opened ears and the locked hasp of mind.
A shape of wholeness focused, revealed.

Here along the riverbank in summer
each second a flowering world, suddenly
an arrow of clarity shot: whatever happens,
with you or not, is perfect, consummate.
The self-sufficient water, smallest leaf,
season's round, prove it over and over.

Skies gamut of light limned in a point,
epiphany both huge and minute as a star,
holding greeting's joy and parting's pain,
realised but hidden, past and now,
impossible, easy, O all-life vision
I take your hand that's never out-of-joint.

                                        ANNE BORN

Winter Evening

Black lace of winter branches
Laid on the pale skin of evening,
Eternity cupped within the moment,
Loneliness shattered by the voice
Of the one great star.

Life makes pause in its rise and fall,
There is a lull between the winds
And in the earth's breathing,
So that the pulse of the Cause may be heard, hammering –
Do not refuse the voice of the Great Star.

                                        MAY IVIMY

After The Darkness

Life
pulsing through my veins
the relief of blood
running, rushing back
notes spilling from my fingers
echoing wildly
the thrill of finding harmony
welling from unpractised hands
yet a deeper knowledge
of earth and river
swells from its source
finds its channel

Waking from sleep
the solid sap in my skull
density of fallen cloud
softens, slowly melts.
Sudden, a gush of breath
clear and lucid
oh the gift!
the heart's shaping of life
clenched in my hands.

And so it was
that my strength returned
I stood up tall
and saw all things clearly;
the earth grew richer
the trees full and heavy
and golden flowers shook
in the sedge at evening.

Live coals in a grate
beat against the rib cage
this

slow rising yet
foundation sure.
I know things at their root
I shall not be dazzled by brightness
nor fall in a dark instant
my arms flexed in bronze
my body arched in light.

ROSEMARY PALMEIRA

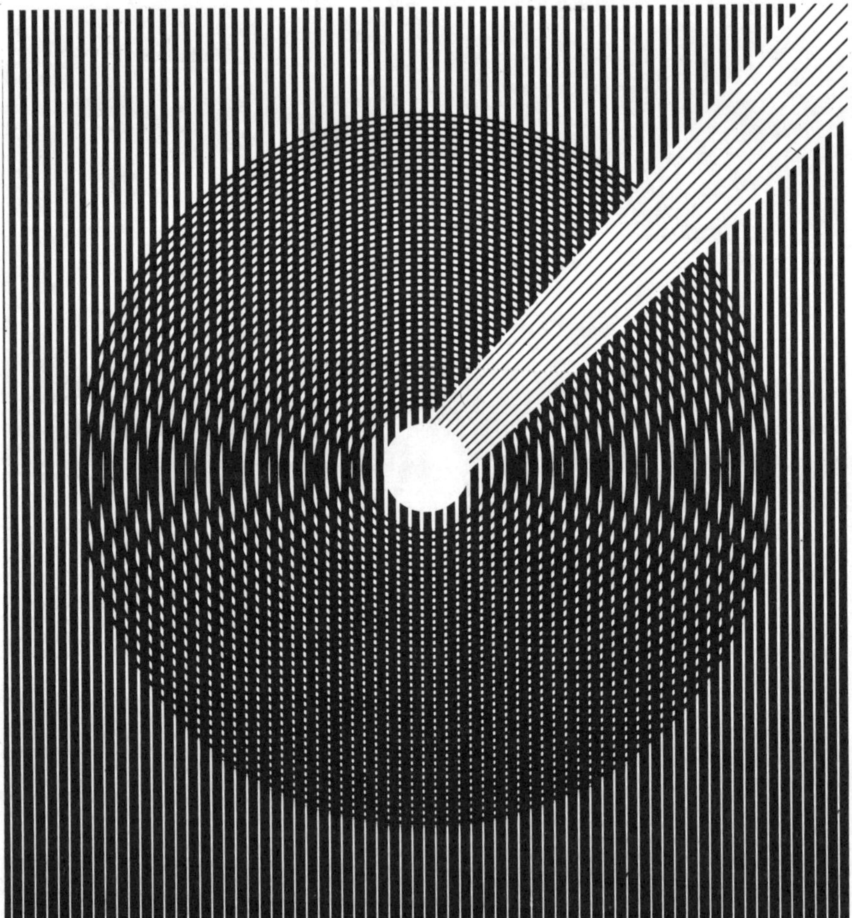

III

INTO ANOTHER WORLD

(air)

No water can vanish my fire
No fire can melt my metal
No metal can cast my mould
No mould can capture my image
No image can reflect my aura

For

I am the dew of the ocean
I am the flash of the darkness
I am the smile of the tear
I am the peak of the depth
I am eternity of the moment
I am the poet

Shruti Pankaj

Creation

He takes a small stone, a dull grey, flat stone and rolls it in his hands, rubs it between his calloused palms. When the stone is warmed he presses a hole into its centre and holds it up between thumb and fore-finger, above his head, and peers through it with one eye clenched shut and the other squinting, as if he were peering through a spy-glass.

He can see clouds moving through the centre of the stone, and the deep blue of the sky beyond. He breathes in slowly, sucking the air through puckered lips, sucking the blue sky through the stone. It catches, and the stone winks its azure eye. He folds his hands around it as if he were cradling a tiny bird, and weaves a silent sealing spell.

No-colour is given colour.

He rolls the stone again now through his hands, caressing it, thawing its ice with his love, pressing and pulling with his strong fingers till it moulds and bends to his touch. He works as a craftsman works, with small flickering gestures, sculpting and smoothing, pummeling the stone until at last he is satisfied.

No-shape is given shape.

He holds the stone gently in the palm of his hand. It lies and gleams in the sunlight. He inhales, long and deep, holding the breath in till it starts a shudder in his belly that ripples out and through him, trembles from his fingers and quivers into the heart of the stone.

The stone sighs. The wings flutter almost imperceptibly. A shiver. The stone wings lift and drop wearily. Wait. He lifts his hands high in the air and thrusts upwards. The stone hovers, then soars. A butterfly. A piece of sky.

No-life is given life.

SARA JONES

Writing A Poem

It is clearly not enough
merely to cover the paper,
to wear the mask of another,
to wallow idly in images,
to sprinkle the metaphors,
to construct a labyrinth
of words and associations.
It is necessary to have
something to say.

If you have something
to say and have acquired
the skill to say it
in your own way,
if the time is right
and the gods are smiling
in your direction, then
out of unending Being
there may emerge
a being strangely familiar:
the essence of your truth,
the poem you always
dreamed of writing.

RAYMOND TONG

Symbols Of Transformation

So few do understand you yet, Carl Jung.
Still we think in feet where you thought in miles.
Light years may travel past before we know
To be transformed, symbols are the only
Proper targets for guns whose golden shells
Are rationalised *Desire*.

DESMOND TARRANT

from Dossiers Secrets (Canto 2)

II

Earth mother goddess squat spread-eagle
        recumbent countryside respite
        marked strategy of circle stone
        of avenues and barrows wood concealed
        unseen for centuries their buried bourne
        unmastered by the micro-chip
        their codes computers computate re-fuse
Each nineteenth year her cycle generates
        a four-square pattern traced on stone
        as transient as fingers traced on mist
Their comprehensible and mystic faith
        researched through practice realized
        a central understanding for their daily chores
        not atrophied to artificial attitudes
        impelled to work a foreign tongue
        compound a way of life another landscape forged
        believe a racist lie a chosen few
        contort a natural dignity to pageantry
        debase the present for a future life

XII

        as a novice hand-led
Joseph descends the cave within the Tor
        drank Keridwen's Cauldron
        thorn apple and red
        birchwood's mushroom skin
        aconite and belladonna
        various fruits and herbs

          the fungi of narcotics
          with a touch of henbane
          delivered by witches
          for the wizards of the countryside
this underground of knowledge
concealed amongst an undergrowth of years
          where spirits pass
          trace avenues above
          the veins of history
his body tranced
detached his senses freed
he moves at will through space and time

                                    SNOWDON BARNETT

from Tarot

1. The Magician

In the garden,
a tree taps
morse warnings
upon my window.

Beyond,
the sky is
tinged yellow.

• • •

She turns
machiavelli –
the beat
of her drum
entrances me.

• • •

As I touch
the moist earth
she whispers.

Warm breath
steams, fastens
about my waist.

2. *The High Priestess*

She is throned on memory,
shrouded in blue passions.

Guidance in moonglamour,
she discards our torches

like dead stars,
extends her hand to lead us.

Now we may walk backwards,
trace the crescent

emblazoned on her cloak
with eyes and mouth tight shut.

3. *The Empress*

The deep night
laps at her,
amber nimbus
clouds
her features.

She brings gifts.
Yesterday she placed
white roses
by my head.

Her hand rested
on my brow
cautious as a moth.

But tonight
I ride out dreams,
she transforms
into crude rock.

5. *The Hierophant*

Iron gates
loom over me,
I am enraptured
by their clangour.

Beyond,
the scent is musty.
Plunging deep among flowers
I grasp a black poppy.

The stem breaks,
a key of sorts.

6. *The Lovers*

The storm passes
overhead,
I taste salt.

Virgin darkness
shrouds us;
weightless,
we break apart

and are swaddled
like new-borns,
like anchorites.

10. *The Wheel of Fortune*

An old woman of Lyonesse
spins the cycles
of my blood.

Yet I am free to weave
her into this web,
even dew-blind
as the spider.

I am led on
by her pumping foot
and the spangle of morning –

until I turn,
snapping crystal threads.

PHILIP KANE

Nightmare

The thunderclap shout at noon
Flings apart echo
And panics the rambler
Into blind flight

The scientist shivers
In the top secret lab
At the unexplained wound in the core

The driver blacks out
On the shimmering curve
As his fender spins off the tarmac

The sleeper dives down through unplugged earth
When his universe drains to a sump

And the rough god
Jumps in the skin
Poised on a trigger
He leaps us from the driving seat
He bucks across the code
His wildness quivers sparks in the molecules
As the sun grows horns

He squats on us fiery as migraine
He shoots us through tearing stampedes
His hooves kick out the budding stars

Acknowledge him.

LES TATE

The Holy Fool

He was a prince once
proud
light-struck, renounced
heritage
now
compelled to the byways.

Not mere expiation his rags
and madman's guise –
the least of all creatures
but an exulting, rejoicing
at all odds, a profound
sharing of pain and love
in the simpleness of man.

This is his role:
to each passer-by
a call to poverty
to the essence of things
to extremity
to life in death.
A discomfort, an insult
like that other stone of stumbling
caller to compassion
become broken for love.

He takes you to the abyss
you stand there shaking
he has survived
you may not.
He takes you to strange lands
you are afraid to follow on.
Wherever he goes
people hold themselves in.

He is unloved, avoided
appalling loneliness
carves his cheeks
but his face is illumined.
Tired, age-old
dazed with pain
yet he understands
the secret heart of things.
He has no gifts, no words
but those who have met him
are blessed
outcast in the world
he walks
in the face of light.

ROSEMARY PALMEIRA

Pilgrim Woman

for Pamela Fenton Marshall
1926 – 1983

This is my map: a square of crumpled cloth,
the continents scratched with my fingernail.
Though far, far out between two worlds
I know where I'm going.

This interim of yellow, fetid dark, clenched
hands, the sweated pain of travelling –
this must be done with soon.

Don't comfort me
don't make me weak.
I need endurance now
to focus
my one deep eye, a red jet burning.
For this I concede confinement, torture.
If I lose resolve
I'll fall to the sea floor, die again
and again, breathe only sour water.

In answer I dream of my landfall,
my horizon-curved ledges
stone warm to the warm skin of my hands and my feet:
a whole, brown-skinned and straight-backed land,
rivers of good, strong blood in me
singing from sun to moon.
Here my lost, uncharted years
hang, lambent fruit, deep
in blue trees of the interior.

I wake to want,
again, to wrench this caul, this blindness
from my head, rise up and use
these wasting bones. Already I
have carved my footprints on the shore.
I want to press my feet deep inside those prints!
I want to shed
my old selves quietly,
emerge
emerald and shining,
jagged as a dragonfly.

Don't touch me:
don't hold me back.
Instead
I step from my body's ship
on to the salty stones.

Safe,
delivered,
triumphant,
everything is before me.

PIPPA LITTLE

Rastaman

See him there,
understand
he is maker of religion.

He is repudiator.
He emphasizes
image of God
in an indelible presence.

Understand,
he restages
a stubborn black man's count.

A bush voice booms
there's no model people,
there's only another face,
another variation.

Understand,
because it is good and pleasant
for brethren to dwell together

his dreadlocks assemble
a garb and warrior gear.
And in his wine of weed
in a drumming in Psalm 133

he stops
Babylon
trampling him.

Understand,
it's no rebel head he rests with:
it's an open treetop
for revelation beyond Reggae.

He'll reclaim
creation
in man walking Westindian.

JAMES BERRY

The Spiritual

Black the star's path
To the village of liberation,
To the place disdained in ourselves.

Black the music of transformation,
Freedom's jazz song;
Let magi, angels, animals, understand

In Bethlehem love is born
With night-folk, the discarded, unrenowned.

BERNARD SAINT

The Magic Coming Of Eclipse Dawns

Isn't it glorious
How the pygmies
Climb the trees
She said
Swaying in the breeze
To collect honey
In South Africa.

The spirit dancer's voice replied
The dark side of your moon is awaiting...

Well the blacks
Are the real children
Of the earth
Sputtered the trendy body dancer
Swallowing down the soap.

The spirit dancer's voice replied
The dark side of your moon
Cannot be reached
By astronauts
In rockets.

The musician sang: Maybe the whites
Are the real immigrants
Visitors from outer space, you know.

The spirit dancer's voice replied;
The dark side of your moon
Is not the eclipse
You are frightened to look into
But the magic coming
Of eclipse dawns.

Perhaps, said the physician
The earth is a meeting place
For blacks and whites.

The spirit dancer's voice replied
The dark side of your moon
Is screaming...

Climb the honey trees
Collect the wisdom
You discarded
When you labelled 'me' primitive

Your full grown blackness
Awaits
Your recognition.

The earth holds
The seasons
Of all branches
In its womb.

The magic coming of eclipse
Dawns...
The dark side of your moon
Will not be reached
By astronauts
      In rockets.

                                LINDA KING

Behind The Cross

By crossing the Christ,
The son of Adam
Might have committed a grave blunder –
But the son of Mary,
Has shone more brightly than the sun –
And shown:
Life is sacrifice,
Not surrender!

By silencing Jesus,
The rod of power
Might have created
The nightmare of injustice –
But the code of life,
Has taught to the world:
Power is not life,
Life is peace!

By mortalising the immortal,
The vanity of flesh
Might have won for the moment –
But the spirit of the soul
Has sung the song of divine love:
Life is eternal,
Life is not a segment!

SHRUTI PANKAJ

The Neverending Journey

(Which led me to understand how straight up-and-down most poems are...)

The journey is
a straight line from
origin to enlightenment and
I walk the line
unswerving
step after step
towards my
vision of
the ultimate

The line becomes
a circle which
contains the journey and
develops within it more
circles
circles within
circles and
all contain the journey
the beginning and
the end

The all is contained
within
the pattern which
begins to pulsate with
life drawing
me into the centre
then out to the
edge the
inner and outer
inner and outer and
all the circles
contain the
journey the
beginning and
the end from
origin to
enlightenment

The truth is
now I
am the answer I
am the end and the
beginning I
am the origin and the
enlightenment and
the heart beat
is the journey through
the pattern which
contains the
journey and
I am the
journey and I
am the
pattern and I
am the
question that
starts the
journey and
every journey is
a circle in
the pattern and
I am the
pattern...

BARBARA S. COLE

from "D'Où Venons Nous? Que Sommes Nous? Où Allons Nous?"

for my children:
(Nicola, Diana, Susan, Sally, Michaela and Mark)

I

The Imperative of Blue

In compliant morning
Up adroit ladders of air
To careful, planned slaughters
Sea-birds
Climb westwardly,

Plunge
      shadowless,
Slice the blue membrane,
Pincer the astonished catch,
Coast possessively away.

The imperative of blue
Is the plunge outward.

Child in the womb
Dives compulsively;
So we must attempt
The seamless waters,
Vague abysses among stars.

Do you remember
How the sky shakes,
Shudders like a swell of sail,
Strains to carry you away with it?

Do you remember
How the sea, hungering,
Veined,
Falls Rises
Like a woman's belly
Accomplishing desire?

This side the edge of sleep
We may not attempt
Fledged declensions of the dream;
Compelled
By the imperative of blue
We must plunge outward.

I have dreamed myself a fish,
Elegant, tight-waisted,
Anonymous
In the safe belly of the sea.

I have dreamed
Quick dexterous beaks,
Hinged intruders,
Unshadowed as a sentence as the innocent;
The astonished gulp.

In whatever sleep I dream
I must not wake but to plunge outward,
Take passage
Upon seamless waters,
Vague abysses among stars.

The blue surrounds
The blue commands.

V

"... in a strange land?" PSALM CXXXVII

In our nights of deep remembering
We forget what we must not forget:
Dreams that we wove with our fears,
Hopes that we raised with our tears,
Words that are words that are words.

In our nights of secret muttering
Each has said to his heart,
Soon I will rise up
Rise up and go swiftly,
Rise up and go over high hills

Over wide plains,
Go naked,
Unashamed,
Go to the new lands.
Like a prophet I will go,
My bare feet bleeding,
My bright eyes burning,
Like a prophet from the Book
To the Kingdom I will go,
Naked,
Unashamed,
My bright eyes burning,
Burning with deep faith.

Each has said to his God
Words that are words that are words.

Yet the new land waits
The new land calls
The Kingdom of God is awaiting
The prophet who dwells in the heart.

Halleluia – hear the voice!
Halleluia – let us sing!
Halleluia! Halleluia!
Hal – le – lu – uu – uu – ii – a!

In my nights of deep remembering
(Domine non sum dignus)
In my nights of secret answering,
In my nights of careful reckoning,
(Domine, Domine, non sum dignus)
Let me not forget,
O let me not forget!

For what I may forget
Leaps in my blood with urgency
And fills my nights with agony,
And what I may forget
Is foremost in my memory:

Dreams that I wove with my fears
Hopes that I raised with my tears
Words that are words that are words
Sins that are sins that are sins.

These I may forget
And go into that land
But half-aware.
But half-aware!

O tortured flame that knows no dark!
That knows no dark – o tortured flame!

                                            A.L. HENDRIKS

The Powers

We don't know what we do, we don't know that,
But: every time contains a sign, like apple seed;
And, if we bite, oh, if we sow by seeing –
A new series is begun
But if energy is low and danger doesn't gleam as challenge,
Then, whether we sit still or run,
The powers come hunting with dog and gun.

They're not after fresh meat, if it's still young,
No, it's the scent of old inertia they have;
They follow gangrene, fear, complaints,
And tear those who should know better limb from limb;
Or some they incarcerate in horrid selves;
And even as you've touched or torn, they wait to see
If there's a turning in you to the true;

and they'll release and heal you if they do;
and set you food, and play a stirring song,
and put you on your way, when you are strong.

ALAN JACKSON

The Lioness

Sitting lazily watchful on her haunches
her sanded skin is strangely soft,
such poise and coolness.

No mocking now,
one careless strike of that paw
could strip the flesh from your cheek.

You may have come to fight against her
but now your better course must be
to sit and match her, stare for stare.

Dare to gain such close arrest
for yourself,
such peace of mind and surety of soul
as you have never hoped to hold.

LIZZIE SPRING

The Sounding Circle

*"an infinite sphere, centre everywhere,
    circumference nowhere."*
                – Hermes Trismegistus

Listening inwardly
I hear a finer singing
like the song of unseen seals
or the distant Sirens of Hellas
caught in the lulls
and pauses of earth's rumour,
in the wider murmur of the sea.

It is rhythmic
as punctual tides
are rhythmic;

it sings of a truth
that was and is
as primordial as death;

not new and never old
it sounds

in the sounding circle.

GLADYS MARY COLES

The Way

Beyond the wandering in the mapless wilds –
                    lost –
in fear, or wonder, swallowed in landscape,

past even feeling the way along the blind line
between the yes and the no in the moment,
as the pure note chimes, or fades –

there is a digging of the strata deep,
        a laying of the stones,
there is the building of a path

that sings through the dark land
of its delight in dancing out
the poem of its pattern to the gods.

                              ANDREA CLOUGH

The Wheel

Let go, be still
be still and know
let spirit speak
to spirit direct
no intervention of
thought or word
climb off your wheel
your thousand rungs
step off the whirling
spokes onto
the still axle
the pivot of turning
step into
the eye of God
discover your own
reflection there
stand at the heart
of all that moves.

                              ROSEMARY PALMEIRA

Villa Di San Michele

I leave the house white with cool shadow
appointed fit for a god,
sculpture, painting, glass, in tamed sunlight;
climb the hill. Lizards
are all that move. Emerald arrows.
I must have been here before
to feel such total connection.
Cruelty – bird-snaring, blood
let by cold Tiberius
spots my scarred hand. Love, among olives,
vines tenderly birthing night-eyed infants,
shakes my womb. The pure blue bay
whose far shore exhales grey breath
from Naples' poverty and joy,
drains Genuario's liquidating veins.
Baby embraced, girl, slave, matron, crone,
more than today's skinflakes
       know this as home.
Crossed the bay to the island, felt as I feel
rolling here and away ceaselessly on time's wheel.

                            ANNE BORN

Arriving Late At The End Of Time

Please follow me, she calls,
To where the sad music is playing.

And of course I rise from my chair.
And I follow her to the first purple edge
Of my darkness.

There is no music. I didn't expect any.
We walk a long way, not touching nor speaking.
Though I can feel her warmth and smell her hair.

We become the very soul of distance.
I suppose a blind man from where he stood
Could guess the smallness of us.

Three more steps, and then... another,
And we are clear of the world.
I turn back to it, because of a sound I recognise.
A music of hearts catching at hearts.

Here, she says. And hands me a bluer flower
Than October can ever give, or any month.
Our smiles touch.

Two minutes after the end of time,
That is all there is. A flower,
And a breathing blueness.

OWEN DAVIS

This Place

I remember a dream where I stood
on a rock, before me the open
sea. There was nothing else there
but the sky.

I thought, no one else can follow
me here, no one can see what I
alone am seeking.

It was you that taught me
about mountains and sun,
taught me that the sun is never
really on the mountain. I remember
walking to that mountain and finding
rock. I walked on and I found
more rock. Then I found what you did
not say. I found that the sun was
inside the mountain.

This place that I have
been to, only I can speak of.

SARAH PEEL

Excabbala

Bedlam smelted to this
Pure Bethlehem metal
My EYE's
Swordgaze guards
The angelic mirror's door.

Its Demangelic
Beauty bolt body caught
Naked there
In the thunderflash of its daring.
Such

Voltage
if it exist how forbid it?
Yet if its power is also genocidal
This is the blade that we must hold now
Steady here between us
Pure Angelsword of
EYE.

HARRY FAINLIGHT

There Were Three

Our beaks have probed
into every crevice
of the human condition.
There is nothing
that we have not seen
or do not understand.
Take heed!
Listen to the ruffling
of our feathers;
observe the tilt
of our eye;
Savour the tensile strength
of our reedy legs.
We are your guides.
Discover in our flowing necks
what you need to know.
Don't hesitate!
Our red toupées are your warning.

CAROLYN ASKAR

Into The Blaze Of Day

Into the blaze of day she comes
my grandiloquent woman
her hands full of mystery, god —
and I sink deep into mind
which I share with those of my kind
where words stutter drunkenly
over greenwet stones and abiding springs,
and life surprisingly sings.

She crosses the room and goes out
into a flowerful, light-emblazoned

garden and I follow in feeling.
Gone into a summer-dozing world
I am left to celebrate
first in a garden tenderly tended,
then in an old lane full of silence
and verdure's leaning leaves,

then by a whispering sea.
To love so is to be sun-maddened
on hard stone beaches and dream
that at the far side of rock or wave
and beyond the deftly coloured world —
I praise the artist in every fibre —
we see the bright god-star gleam
dark at noon, lighter than any light.

WILLIAM OXLEY

The Healer's Art

for Su

A royal flush of revived spirits
A hand packed with the metaxy
Of ghosts and familiars,
Good weather at the fingertips.

She deals a winning hand
Into the leaden skies
That depress the movement
Of joint and ligament.
She makes a pass and the sun
Breaks through; she palms the pain
And brings out the true grain of the hurt.
She has a lightning-crackle
About her own skin that jumps
Through the deadened gristle, so that
The joint once more feels its spring.

And the unwelcome ghost that slips
From the shivering man,
As the surfacing sulphur
Of a fever, is touched
In a royal handshake.

The ghost turns to momentary
Egg-white in her fiery palm,
And is gobbled by the salts
Issuing from her fingers.
Then she shakes hands with herself
Under running water,
And the spirit of the fever
Is stitched into the rainfall
That has run through the healing
Copper of the plumbing,
Meeting with the other rivers
Of the town's flushed garbage,
A confluence of unwanted ghosts
Pulled out to deepest sea.

ALAN BLEAKLEY

Air

Ocean-skin can cream and curdle
Like a leaden custard stirred from below.
Spray-spikes can grow out of calm
And high drowning greens, drawn by moons.

So can air, with knobs and yieldings, drown.

To walk through air as though it has no surface
Is to be ill from smallness

No fungus'd stump, or house-
Stones that turn to moss

Calls their change loss.
But how can any element console
A man, always on fire,
Who calls ash failure?

Tell him, oh
Tell him, there is no disaster –
And no dove! That in a shoal
Of powers that move as one
Fish, that scatters, reforms
– A storm within storms
He is, a mariner of air

Who wrongly thinks himself a lone fish there.

P.J. KAVANAGH

The Poetry Of Birth

for Goolden

Let these words bear the sound
of a name being born

like ordinary
sunshine or rain falling
on the silence of a thought

like conversations
stretching back in a stare
which cannot be heard.

Are you listening?

Are you listening?
from the sea or the stars?

This birth will occur
like the moon floating
into the sky
higher than a reaching hand

and be reflected
in water uncatchably,
on fingers trailing
as it passes by,

the crystal-clear sound
about to make shore
in invisible words

crying like gulls,
repeating one name
along the horizons.

GEOFFREY GODBERT

Doubt Not That We Shall Found The City

Doubt not that we shall found the city,
the time of waiting is nigh, preparations are at hand.
Self healing is accomplished not by one but by many.
You are all brothers and sisters in God.
You already know the truth
it is always at the kernal of life.
The process is towards a greater clarity in each and everyone.
There is no divide.
You have to learn to stand firm in the spirit
among/under all circumstance.
The founding depends on this.
This shall be the foundation,
there shall be no other.
Do not doubt the truth is firm within you.
This time is the uncovering of this truth.
From this all else will flow.

The crystal stone speaks of the deep silence beyond time
wherein the spirit has its source.
The spirit is not separate from you,
this is also your source,
wherein you all shall dwell.

The stone face speaks of all that is prior.
It speaks of patience and the waiting
prior to the knowledge of the spirit
where you shall dwell.

'Tell me about the foundation.'

It is not of one but of many,
not by one alone may the stone be raised.

'Tell me about the foundation.'

The foundation stone is the incorporation of revealed truth
not of one but of many.
The foundation is the spirit made flesh in time.
The flesh in time enables the spirit to move.
Without this it is static and has no movement,
nor can it speak.

'That is why I was angry at your immobility, at your lack of action.'

You did not understand this. The spirit exists outside of flesh.
The spirit is in the air you breathe.
It is in the sight of your eye,
in the sounds of your ear.
It breaths through your touch.
It is not separate in any way.
To pray is to open to the spirit in time.
To incorporate is to exist in time,
wherein the purpose.
The purpose is the seed of its own fulfilment.
You carry the seed of your own fulfilment
of the purpose of the spirit,
so that it may move in time,
though it exists beyond time.
This is the meaning of,
'Thy will be done'

2

'Speak to me of the foundation.'

It exists in time but its effect shall be –
has always been – outside of time.
Others will come who know this to be true.
You are not alone.
The spirit is uncovering.
It is the work of the spirit to uncover.
This is the meaning of
'Bring to birth.'
It is an opening – flowering –
all that is before the opening,
is simply before the opening.
The spirit cannot flow
until the opening has been achieved.
You already know what is to be done.
You simply uncover it.

'Why can't you reveal this?'

The state of uncovering should be experienced in time,
though the move towards the uncovering,
the source of that movement,
exists outside of time.
You are not separate.

Each step must be experienced to fully understand
the uncovering.

'Tell me about truth and illusion.'

The truth is the spirit, illusion is the state before the uncovering of the spirit.
Everything that dwells in life is incorporate spirit.

'Are you of the golden people?'

Yes I was with you then.

Tell me about 'I'.

I am spirit.
I am not incorporate spirit. I am not you yet we are not separate, for in spirit there is no separation. Separation is not possible. Only before the uncovering of spirit, is it possible to believe this. This is because spirit is covered, as the stones were covered.

'Were you there at the uncovering of the stones?'

Yes you saw me.

'How?'

Not with eyes but in the uncovering of the stones, did you see.
The stones incorporate spirit within a larger time
but they speak what is outside of time.

'Do you know how difficult this is now?'

It is hard for me to see. There is a lot to be done. I am here to guide you. You must help me on this.

HILARY NORMAN

What We Choose To See

Light streams over the ledge of the globe
from out of darkness;
blinding whiteness of crystal waterfalls.

Opaque droplets of shimmering intelligence,
pour into bone-dark cavities of life,
turn blood-red cells to milk-white rivers
of seed and nourishment.
Cuckoo spit oozes from a leaf.
Ice-caps melt to release snowdrops
growing to white hyacinths, lilies:
– a layette, bridal gown and a winding sheet.

Whitening mushrooms thicken inside skulls;
brilliance gathering under tinted filters
occasionally spills in a smile, look or action:
his heart a sea-foam of caring,
her dove, rising from the waves, white-winged.

Chequer-boards, we move through our squares.
Black and white are one, and both are in the rainbow
– according to a Rasta friend.
What we choose to see, is, by our choosing.

CAROLYN ASKAR

The Caravan

Only now do I feel and see the nuances of light
with so much ripe and resting before it will burst outwards,
there is mellow blue which is almost, not quite, soft as you
but it is darkness which wraps as carefully as you, and as bright.
We are holding the balance between two far ends of life,
between is a rhythmic flow of juice-carried energy
and more, movement and more, heart-talk and more, much more.
The centrepoint of you is fine-edged as a knife.
Soon will come the urge to break out into a rush of feeling,
the pulsing of unearthly bodies will impinge on our bodies,
and at the end of the caravan a man will be happily reeling.

DAVID STUART RYAN

The Second Coming Over Lindisfarne

1.1

In the magnificats of the morning
my soul cannot but bow
      before Thee,
           O Morning-Star
Brilliant, alleviant, out-riser of the dawn –

And the dawn will emerge from the Earth
of the night, the dawn will rise
flushed with a thousand thankfulnesses

For the night's embrace – the dawn will rise
as she here rises, steadfast over the
low horizon upsings her heralding soul –

And my heart sweeps out to sea – with
the dawn wind sees in the silver-blue
such gleams of its own purity – now

in song upraises again to greet your gaze

O morning-star, O brilliant lambent flame –

1.2

And the onrolling momenta of the morning
are beginning to emerge gleaming like
scallops for the shore – gleaming like
star-strewn fish-scales played by
the lyre of the wind, who weaves
swiftly five thousand leagues full of
blue into silvery fleeces of cypress,
or high, high skein of sky-honking geese –

Here the morning is singing, the stars are cymbals
clashing in the still of night and the great
golden morning-star outwinks them with
ardour – burns like a heart from
the hall of the morning, high to the dawn –

O Dawn, o softly stealing lieder to dissolve
my antagonisms – o musical adagio,
colorous asker for my heart – you have me,
hold me to you – dawn, I am yours –
made of the same amazement, rose –

Flush with the whispering skies weave
the sea's hollow transparencies
flush with the rock's unbreakable
shadows stream and gleam the
silent immeasurabiles of foam –

These rocks are my home – this Earth,

My house – my giver – In her I live

The great soul of Christ stretches
like an Angel over Lindisfarne, but
one rock-line cared for, carved
carried in the lamps of His lantern –

And the train gathers on, gathers on over
the steel rails glides to where Berwick
is sleeping under the wing of His Angel,

Him –

How love gathers to a tear-sob
                for the frailty of the thing –
                          the sleeping town –

How love gathers,
               how love hallows –
Held in the heart of night,
            Held to the heart of Light –

Held in Him who is
        All-Hallower –
         All-Wholer –
          All-Who –
Living YOU
                of God –

        1.^{3}

How God goes through these humans
wholly – the whole town –

First in the Thrones
            who thrive in the limbs

Then Cherubims
            whole-seers

    Seraphims
            through-weavers

Firers of love –

How full shall they live who know Him –

How live shall they feel who Him know –

Him how whom they love shall He fill –

                          CHARLES LAWRIE

New Age

for the Sisters at St Michael's Convent, Garston

It is coming –
From high in the light where it begins
It is coming –
See the Earth rising to meet it
It is coming –
This long slow harvest of centuries
It is coming –
With a voice like the bell of a trumpet

Dawn of Aquarius, dawn of light
Bird of mid-summer hovering in the sky
Dovebird firebird angel bird
Filling the sky's circle
High across its stretched inner blue
Up above a child's uplifted face
The Earth rising towards the bird
The Earth in light turning in space
This blue pearl planet radiating light
Spinning in a single ringing note
The Earth is turning to, yearning to, returning to

Deep in this quiet place
I find my hands brought together
I hear a voice saying 'ask and receive'
I feel what it would be to doubt no longer
I see my arms opening up above my head
Holding the light in a vertical shaft of air
As it comes down flooding the silence
My skin tingling like a tuning fork
My head held back as I call out *I am here*
My body walking forwards towards a line
Coming to meet him on the other side
Where the ground breaks – and I can only jump
In faith – with nothing but this
Bared first and last self I am left with

That soul-spark I know
That invisible clear face in your face
Voice in your voice, that can trust
That can let go – and so simply
This lifelong rightness in our hearts
That can dare to say yes, it is true
I know why we are here, I can remember
I can remember the time I was grass
I can remember my first breath out of water
I can still see the starlight in your eyes
And know that you know in your innermost
Child that is stirring to reawaken us
Touched in the morning light
By the sun on the grass and the sky's clear
Blue you quicken to, dress and go out
Into this hour of Creation

Day stretching out all sun on the seed of you
Lying out on the mother ground
With nothing to do except be: the Garden
Be birdsong woodsmoke rose-smell bee-hum
Be the joy of breaking into a run
Be the wonder of taking the word flower
And watch it turn back into a flower
Into the thing it always was and is
And I am, and you are, at last – alive
Light-filled and wild
And home from home

Dawn light
River of light
Flowing into life
The light in your eyes
The light in your heart
You speak to me from
As I turn to return:
'Illuminate your life'

Now it is time to begin
To live our real lives out from within

✧

World shadow spread across the ether
This spiral of light is descending to –
Filling your human eyes as your head bows
Where you stand on this darkening ground of air –
The Night of the World Soul swirling, suspended
Its satellite images of suffering flickering
From synapse to synapse: this last reality
Yoked, dragging its effigy out to this edge
Wheeling in the round of its crowded myriad
We were all of us one by one born to –
The wasteland we all carry only we can change
This lifeless myth we have all lived
And hardened into droning form –

And this is the gravity which holds us here
This is the paradox: every thread of this
Loom is what we have lived to weave
To come into the depth we have the only way
That has left us to finally come of age
And choose to live what we were made for –

Borderline we can only reach in time
Now the old world is beginning to die
As the light comes down into our lives
Into our days and nights and dreams

And as it comes, the shadow rises
Towards its apocalypse, the nadir
Mirroring us to ourselves in pain and rage
At the abuse and misuse – turning you
Back on yourself and your own dead skin
Sucked in to see where it also begins
And the deeper your desire reaches
The clearer you want to be, the more
The heart becomes the only real place left –

Heart born out of light and dark
And only heart that can crack the shell
Our hearts are caged in – heart we come to
As we crumble, and the shadow begins to fall
Into the cry of birth that is our soul's
Come alive as if for the first time
Each time –

God, I can feel, I can breathe
I can stand, I am – and in compassion
I can stand on fire with my heart open
I can make my pain my cleansing
I can see the shadow of my suffering

I can see the world's shadow
Becoming a rainbow – and I am
Holding this small globe between my hands
And there is light heat coming
Out from the centre of my palms
God, and my tears are shining

The rainbow needs me
The Earth my tears
The light
This cry
Of joy!

⟡

In the dream, you said
You stood out under the stars
Filling your eyes as you slowly turned round
Alone out there in the dark that was not dark
But alive with starlight and your slow dancing
And as you moved you began to hear them sing
They filled your ears with a wave of sound
Sweeping across the face of the sky –
And one star you began to see
Drawing the sound towards itself
As it closened and brightened, you began to rise
You saw your body standing back
Your body rose around you like mist
Diving up through your arms into the air
The starlight star-sound you became
As the sky blazed with colour, streamed with colour
Flooding the length of you as you flew

And as your voice first came to me in light
Having died, you said, *right through my head*
I turn away, I turn away from death
You came like flame down into my heart
I sang your name out in light, my love
And my whole body became a heart

And now as I stand in my seeing
Under this open secret the sky is holding
In the sun behind the sun, eye behind my eyes
The sound comes down into my voice out of
That the living flame of the Word breaks through

We are the bridge where the worlds meet
We are the Spirit made manifest
Its essence the subtle form we are standing in
Reflecting the visible meaning of anything
In us, as us, and through us as it is
We are everything we have forgotten
We are here to remember and re-begin
People of God – we *are* God
When I say, my friend, I believe in you
Seeing your face in its feeling fineness
Feeling that light you have brought
Uniquely to life in each cell of you
Our being, freed from its chains, its dying
Is passionate realization – we have come
To live what is ours, to bring it through
And rise like the ground within us
Up through our hearts, heads, hands and eyes
This is a generation to end all generations
This is the place and this is the time
And when I know what we can be, I am alive
I can see: we are the poem, we are its prophecy

WE ARE THE RAINBOW
SCORED ACROSS THE THUNDERCLOUD
WE ARE THE TREE OF LIFE
AND THE DESERT AROUND

WE ARE THE CAUSE
WE ARE THE SEED AND THE SEA
WE ARE THE FUTURE
WE HAVE ALWAYS BEEN

And as the scales hang in the balance
The building shakes as the air crashes past
Your voices eclipsed in the middle of the Mass
The wind rising in the bird-scattered trees
The warrior casting his arms outstretched
The healer's concentration unbroken
The child sitting silent and cross-legged
The hill where we stood in sunset silhouette

Let us pray out loud
Say it out loud
THIS IS OUR BIRTH AND OUR BREAKING
THIS IS THE CHOICE WE ARE MAKING

Atom... to molecule... molecule... to cell
Cell... to living tissue... tissue... to heart
Going into the heart... veins and capillaries
Arteries and lungs... brain and skeleton
The heart beat in me –
The heart beat beside me –
From chair to chair lined around the room
And beyond as far as each of us could reach
As I saw us standing forward in a circle
Surfacing to meet each other's eyes
Awed in the presence of who we really are here

Your voices become a wave of light
Breaking on my naked shore
A deep gold light where I walk
My feet in its ground become this ground
And all fear all aching thought all burden
Released in the clear sung calm of its strength
Seeping in through the pores of my skin –

And when it comes, when it begins
In a long horizontal flash like lightning
The Earth spins into –
At the moment of birth
Imagine
Everything gone silent
Our steps as if weightless
Our eyes without need of speech
Our minds pulsating
Our thoughts as one
Stunned act of music
Waking slowly from the grass
I am flung down onto
And meeting you
The whole of you
At last
For real
For this
And yes

We have come through.

✧

The prophecy is now: we have work to do.
The Lovers stand with The World between them
The white heart of the rose is open
And she leans, seventeen, ageless, Virgin
Mother with the crown of her hair radiant
Swept in streaks of electric red green and gold
Holding our world to her
Inward gazing serenity –
As you cry your tears of newness, and sadness
The violin of the Passion pierces through to –
The heart that gathers and reaps you
Threshes, sifts, grinds and kneads you
Into a finer and finer wand that vibrates
In the longing we have to return and heal
The wound that is inseparable
From the duende of your song.

The Age of Light is beginning
We will see the Mind of Creation
We will meet our guides and helpers
And talk with the reality of angels –
And the way is wayless and broken and long.
Faith is the mystery, daily in this waiting
Our greatness is also that we are nothing
We are alone, we are free. To choose, risk
Renew, unendingly, life – without even knowing
What you will live to be now –
As I make my pledge and cross this line
To let go of what doesn't stand in the light
To open my heart to the will of God
To hear the born self cry I am here
All my life and death, I am here

And the summer rain falls on the grass
Behind this high screen of trees
Where you come back down to things as they are
Where it filters down like water through rock
Into the mortal earth.
And still light is bitter and unleavened,
Light is angry: is holy fire,
Full with seeing – and beyond all comprehending
Its source is almighty compassion.
And the full-leaved tree sheds its leaves
Dark red and falling –
The tiny white figure hangs
On the black cross… and you are smiling.
Wake, child, in the morning light
Wake, child, through the door into life

Barefoot on the grass, embracing you.

JAY RAMSAY

A Testament

In memory of B.B.

Unlooked-for, the messenger,
But punctual to our need, reminds
Of who we are, why here,

And of the forgotten
Left so long ago, that those draw near
Who travel far in time.

A scholar, a friend, though seldom seen,
Like-minded, human as I,
Wrote, before the end,

Of how, resisting and incredulous,
From death's reality to this
Real or unreal time and place

Back to a ward where cancer-patients die
His soul was dragged unwilling from its bliss.

Fine books he had written, but this
Last testimony of a learned man who cared no longer
For whatever a life's hard-earned honourable achievement was

Tells how soul longs only to resume
Its true eternal form, that boundless sphere
Without circumference
Whose infinite centre each for ever is.

KATHLEEN RAINE

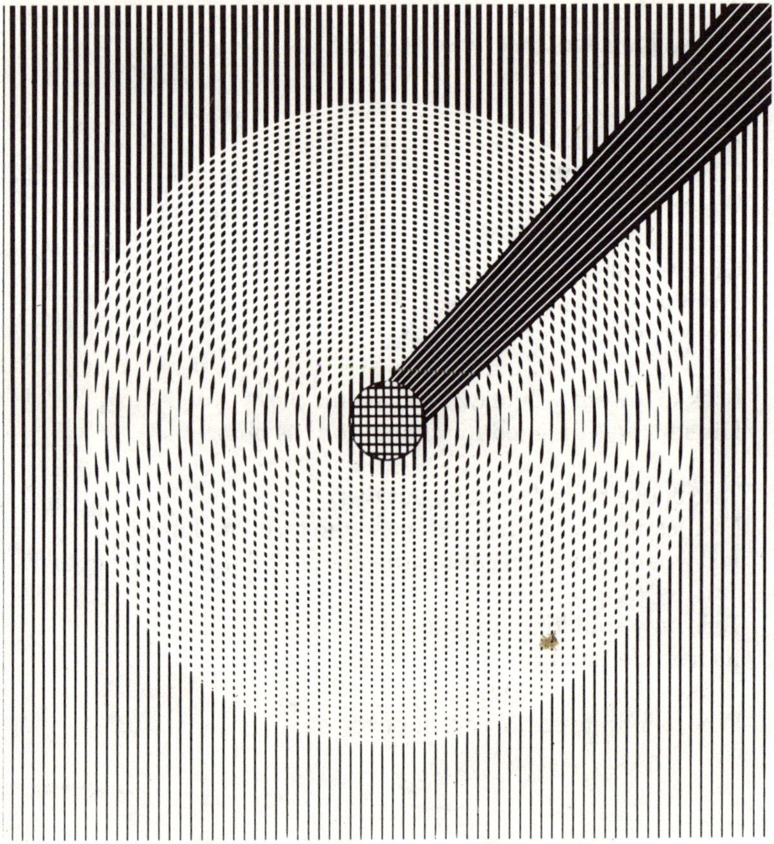

IV

RESURRECTION & RETURN

(earth)

Incarnation

Allow for the fact that
The soul is a cheetah,
*   flashing and swift,*
*   that finds life*

Difficult in captivity:
It hears across the land
*   the running of flanks*
*   on familiar dust*

By the fierce mouthside
The long black strands
*   are melancholy.*
*   Not that it should*

Avoid the condition,
Refusing to fix
*   in the mindblasting,*
*   miraculous chamber*

Where spirit meets grit
For the first time,
*   like tumbled stone.*

Lanny Kennish

Return To Earth

Return to earth
and the sky sings
openness to me
and the ardent ancientries of trees
burgeoning with my beauty
are the young of my ever new eternity's years
as the seagull wings the fluted air
through whispered essences of silence
unsealing synchronous poetries of landscape into mind,
too long sepulchred and starved
in the anti-magic lands
of cities too close to the dead;
those harried Babylons of the robotic spawn
phantoms in the ambience of stress
liquid seething of all seeking time
moving without sight through the very void of the heart
where beats our ever fullnessing of force
so real, so presencefully where we are.

Though Babylon has taught me
the truth the Buddha saw
when he emerged from the palace
from the laps of the dancing girls,
to see the old man
the dying man
and the dead man;
that life is not made for dreams
but only for the wound of waking.

Vain, uprooted flower,
chimera of passion
and power
in despair;
this is man
my forebear.

I have come here
to the old canal
to incandescent water that silvers to the sea
because I have forgotten my heart,
that my belonging's here
belonging nowhere but everywhere,
where the grass roots deep in mystery
and my life
not locked in barricades of brain
and the always breaking body
fragile as a poignantly quivering thread
between the scissors,
throbs and surges the green exaltancy
in the strong of the oak's trunk
and runes in the fierce poetries
of the last flaming of the leaves
where the young god in his alchemies pyres and dreams
of death in his autumnal shrouds of gold.

Simply to remember
if only for a moment without mind
I am nothing
but this river and these trees
I know nothing in my heron-soul,
am master of no-one
not even myself;
is to begin to be healed
of the fathomless audacity of my conceit;
that I create this world
for me in my image,
yet must stand back from my creation
as from the spellbind mirror of my mind
confounded and recoiled and aghast
at my own game.

To let all things be
permit them

to be presenced
as I allow myself
to be presence;
to reclaim the swan to my feeling
as I surrender to the heron's heart,
is to be whole
absorb the part
the parasite that thinks its all upon this planet;
and know I am complete
no need to seek for anything.
No one is separate from the trees.
This is my peace
my only peace
though the dual world
duels and flares and fizzles to its end
on the flailing fuse
through all the never-were wars of separate selves
striving to destroy all otherness
and consume all to a unity
of mind
that is already
our eternity at heart.

ALAN RYCROFT

Aubade

For you

       awakening
your smile
on my lips

         smiling back
to where
a tender tongue-kiss
down – inside
our saliva
of dreams conjoined
glistens
then listens
in a snail's path of a s sounds

                        to

early birds stirring
– first faltering
then trilling
so serenely
such sibilant
song sketches,
they seem to echo
shy rumours of
hitherandthithering
skeins of first sunlight

                       un-

winding, wafting
like webbed waves
at the walls,
lapping
then dancing
like our tongues
round the bed
gently flickering –
lighting up
flames of birdbright high
heartburst w x s sounds

                          – sketching
then etching
veins of new air
                as of angels
casting night from the sky
winging day through each tree
and window and chimney,
ceiling and stair
– dibbling deep dyes of rose
on aethereal gold sheen
melting mists to new green:

like a sainted medieval spirit
winding fresh flowers
through the black death
dawn
        hits
                town

till God's bloodshot eye
rolls higher, wide open –
bathed clean
to shine fiery but twinkling
azure and clear white,
settling heaven's delight
on the dew-dappled dazzle
of new found ground

– breathing again, now
heaving with sound – gathering
word sounds and work sounds –
thrum of wheels, countless
footfalls, doors opening
to sun-stippled leaves
quick with shadows
– now darting
                now still

   like the shadows
     of your hair
        playing light
           on your cheek
just barely re-
   touching
      your shimmering
         smile

on my mouth, on
   these fingers – all
      over my face
     and body
                so gladly

awakening
              with you

                          MICHAEL HOROVITZ

Morning

morning;
in my bowl
green light.
sky burns
turns through
blue silence.
every real sound
falls
on open ears.
i go down now
to the sea
without doubts.

                          STEF PIXNER

On Sighting The First Bluebell

for Chaucer

My eye is my heart
I cannot go further
Bluebell
breaks
the sticky sap heals
at once a dream of waking
the Bell has its safe place
easily sliding between showy shoots
Blue present of early May
I smell the Blueness of it
quite returned.

                                        ELAINE RANDELL

Where Beauty Lies

The Rhododendrons accept
all sadness into themselves
then render it back changed
with a purple glow.

If I could risk that. Love.
And not be shy.
Then I'd walk in the garden
and give sadness away –
to the Chaffinch, to the Gate,
to this bright Laburnum here
so yellow and beautiful,
so beautiful and dangerous.
Ah, that's what I'm on about.
It's risky where Beauty lies.

Surely in Spring we dare
like the flowers be beautiful.
They do not shy.
They shout look at me look.
They are wide open.
And we if we do dare
can gaze into the heart of it,
like the bee, into the pollen,
and be covered all over.

And yes shall I risk it?
to be plunged in, to be entirely
beautiful in the garden
and along the paths
and into the secret heart
where the Caterpillar
spins in the sunlight
and the Rose
shows no shame at all
for its blatant flowering.

Shall I risk
sharing these words with you?
What if I cried?
You will gaze
into the heart of me.
And I am shy
of being seen
to be beautiful.

PAUL MATTHEWS

Three Plants

And this is truly beautiful.
Three plants step up
they countrify a wardrobed town.
Shall I take them singly.

This one has shining hearts
out of the tropical tangle
I could eat their richness but
let us harmonise

night into day
breathing our opposite airs and
I am your dancer
watch me come out go in

so much skin
I would slide against you
is only my fantasy
for your space is perfect

needing no human collusions.
And you hidden high
so many blades falling
I shall not stiffen you.

Let's all make a free fall
and weeping shall not be part of it.
To me you are soundless,
feelings are a constant sight

they sweep in a graceful curve
and how their points
listen to the earth,
even in a tangle

they are all arcs.
And highest seeming dullest
sadness for you.
Not blind hope may lift

that crowded skirt.
Up highest of all one leaf is oiled and free
the face is handling me a splayed laugh
and love can do a lot

to re-organise.
All these hands need is a lift.
And let me say air is everywhere,
listening to air

places me back in myself
and green leaves
moisten my eyelids.
No touching

but the connection of seeing
this moment is all leaves
and in my eyes
they are free to be.

SARA BOYES

The Party In The Woods

I

Each fly a little Isis,
A transformer, buzzing;
The trees worried by their wolf,
The wind. The spring of water,
An almost silent work, continuing
Under the threshold of sleep.
The little rivers of gnats.

II

The boy showed us a pleasant trick,
Taking his pennywhistle to the gnatswarm,
Which widened to the low notes like the outline
Of a Russian Doll that can never be
Overturned completely, and stretched up,
Whirling faster, like a skinny spindle
To the high scales, and with the music
The sunshine shone through every small
Illuminated body.

III

Sometimes we went the long way round,
By the ferry, just to get on the water
For ten minutes. A little spring
Had overflowed into the road
Making a sheet of mirror our tyres unzipped,
And this was as good to her as a festival,
Anything to do with water, falling water,
Flowing, anything, and the shower.

IV

We were not the first at the party in the wood.
The small dark woman in the great hat
Was sitting by the sheet on which the food was spread,
Waiting. The gnat-boy was one of her eight, the youngest.
Then there was the water-woman already mentioned
Who needed water to keep sane, and was beautifully so,
Who would sometimes walk in her street clothes straight into the shower;
Was, due to her use of water, the wife of her lover
(As he slept in their wooden house, he could hear always
The stream-work playing beneath his senses,
Sharpening them, sharpening them, for her).

V

After the picnic they made an expedition
To the old salt-cured casino on the railway-line,
Its salons half-drifted knee-deep up to the tables with sand,
Like crowds of players converted in their souls
To diamond dice, and standing on each others' faces
To follow the exhausted wheels, which was
Their spoil of the game, to be this fractured glass,
And their only speech the rubbing of this harsh talk
Which has so beautifully scoured the wooden house.

VI

Then there was a black man who dropped in when we were playing ghosts;
He put the sheet on in the dusk; and as it was too African a ghost,
Gibbering too much, my wife whisked it off,
But there was nothing underneath. No one saw him leave.
Everyone commented on the whiteness of my shirt,
From a distance they could not tell, they said,
Whether it was a radiation or a garment, and my approach
Was not frightening, with a hovering smile, my shirt
Falling like clean sleet from my pleasant laugh.

VII

She sung to us, the mother of eight,
Who has since stopped singing, like the demolition
Of old beloved places; her husband Luke had brought
His new wife, who might have passed for his daughter.
The two women tenderly embraced, the younger
Having brought wine and flowers, while he,
As if in affirmation of his new state,
Had grown his hair long, it was glossy
And black as eagle feathers, while she,
The mother of eight
Seemed thereafter to have no other state, no song.

VIII

Each fly a little Isis, a transformer
Singing its god-name over the picnic.
We fell to, and after, let them have it.
And the spring of water always singing.
I call my nearly invisible ghost to sing,
That which is black on black within, and strong,
Stronger than I am, sitting by the sheet's hem
Spread on the grass, held by the feast,
Helpless with love of the party, and of each one
Alive or dead who that day came to it.

PETER REDGROVE

Chrysalis

Like all mothers
I gave birth to a beautiful child.
Like all mothers
I wiped myself out,
vanished from the scene
to be replaced by a calm practical robot,
who took my face,
used by bones and blood
as the framework
over which to secure
her carapace of steel, silicon and plastic.
I was locked out of her clean carpentry
and smoothly-reprimanding metal.

Yet that robot's rude heart
flowed with love's essential fuel

because my child was one of the millions
of beautiful children
and knew how to tackle the machine.
She embraced the robot woman lovingly
each day
until her circuits and plastics wore away.
Now the soft real skin can grow,
the blood and breath move again,
the android is banished.

I emerge from the chrysalis
and go forward with my child
into the warm waters of the sea
in which we are both born at last,
laughing, undamaged,
bathing alive in this salty blue,
my motherhood born out of her,
her woman's name and noon out of me.

PENELOPE SHUTTLE

Time

for Zoe at her 5th birthday

She asks me, "What is time?"
and I say it is tomorrow and yesterday,
then and now.

Like the sculptor gouging the clay
or a brick layer laying the bricks
row by row

slapping the trowel down
smoothing
and wiping away excess
making serpentine curves
or even lattice work.
Or barn raising.
Or quilting.
Giving a shape to and making.
Observing the way.
Watching the earth turn.
Or shaping the stone.
Or letting the dough rise.

"I will not be unhappy when you die,"
she says.

Now we are drilling the soil
carefully placing the seeds.
Weeds grown profusely –
Deadly Nightshade.

"Why will it kill me?"
she asks over and over again.

Like a potter turning the world
building and finding the right glaze.

She wants to be a Princess or a Bride.

"What is time?" she asks. "What is time?"

Then and now, I say.
Yesterday, tomorrow and today.

BARBARA ZANDITON

Bringing The Geranium In For The Winter

Almost dark, the rain begins
again. I steal into my own
October garden

with a small black bucketful of
compost and a trowel.
I kneel

as if you, beautiful
before time with your small pale flowers still
opening, were my soul

and God,
in spite of groundfrost
and the book of rules for growing,

could
exist, incomprehensible, companion of
the overcoming darkness in the grass and apple garden.

I return among the small grave stones
I made your borders with
to kneel, to feel

about, to, probing, put my trowel in, pull you from
your unmade bed,
your mad

dishevelled garden: lifted out of,
orphaned bit of
truth

your petals wet with
rain. It's rain I somehow am
no longer stiff with

now my hands
the barest hands I have
are briefly of this earth and have begun

to learn the part of
root and leaf
to live

with
potting and repotting.
So I set

you, lastly, in the dry
companionable kitchen
on a plate,

my table
laid with cloth of quiet
October light.

GILLIAN ALLNUTT

Wolstonbury

    Of hills upheaved into
Peace – His rest
Mighty as His labour.
In whose valleys,
Echolessly as broken pottery,
Men cough,
        plough.

Chimneysmoke for its daylong humility is allowed now
Into higher regions;
A plane at the day's perihelion grinding
Sharp the silence
        – edge to which,
Upon the air's altar,
I offer up this breath.

> In the West, dusk

Opening up a healing-space;
Upon the furthest train's abrasions laying
Its behometh balm
> — O lamb of breath.

The deepest places lie open now;

Are tendered;

Necklaces of distantly shunted wagons
Taken off and lain aside.

HARRY FAINLIGHT

Elegy For Sally

Creator withhold the secret
Till we sufficiently age,
But I can think now
Only of beginnings;
For the end of it we took
With our first breath
And have come to understand
Endings just a little.

You've walked through a key-hole
We all must learn to walk through;
That you've gone where that key-hole takes us
Makes the certainty we'll follow sweeter.

Whisper of sound nearly no sound.
Candle on the carpet flickers,
Incense bends, breaks, re-forms,

Big shadows breathe strange figures at the wall.
Midnight, one – no sleep comes.
Car-door slams, voices climb out of the street,
Drift & die among dark trees
Dipping up into a purple sky.
High there on the precipice of night:
A honey-coloured moon,
A scatter of stars.

In the towns of Death are many windows.
We who dream that we are living,
Peer through them, a sense of something beautiful
Playing with the edges of our hearts,
Though mind fury that those windows refuse
To emanate anything but this one black light
& the mewing of some fog-horn impossibly far away,
A shell's sound, the sound at that moment
Of greatest stillness, the cataract sound
Of our own blood, racing us to what destiny
Immense as a pin-head in these whirling nebulae,
Our fierce home.
O the confusing simplicity of this leaf,
Dried & fallen from the vase! That moon!

Peace,
Peace upon you;
Who'll tell us what kingdoms you inherit
Whilst we swallow blink & cough,
At traffic-lights ensnared,
Amongst fragments of ourselves ensnared,
Fragments of reality fallen by chance into our hands.
We have ear-wigs & wood-lice & our dark brown dreams
To draw conclusions from,
You – have the stars within your breast.

Hushed now every bird but the phantom owl
Soaring low out of the wych-elm
Across spider-web grass woven
Over ancestral grave-mounds.
Rippling waters. Round stones.
A confluence of streams by moonlight.
Sand-bars. Ashes of camp-fires
In the gathering snow.

A light shed into the human soul
From a sky beyond this darkened sky;
A lantern moving along the upper floor
Of an ancient house,
The stabled mare uneasily shifting.

Power wing down,
Patience freely flow;
Exactly where the world ends
The nightingale is singing
Its most tender song.
We are healed in no other way.

Blood resumes its toil
Of lifting magic
To the fleeting heart.

OWEN DAVIS

For All Who Fell In Wars Within And Without The Heart Of Man

The butterfly
above his head
made the sleeping soldier
think the enemy was near

*

bullets rained upon the earth
and flowers were exiled from their stems

bombers scarred the sky with fear
and birds migrated into their wings

gases flooded death into the sea
and fishes got up on their fins and prayed

and men with guns growing out their hands
were too afraid to touch how frail each other was

*

when flowers catch bullets in the wind
and napalm deflowers the dawn
let one soldier become a child again
and make his gun a reed
for butterflies to rest on

when machine gun baby screams
in the cradle of fire
let one soldier become a child again
and fill his helmet with grasses
for sparrows to nest in

when shrapnel blossoms spring
in the path of the yellow reaper
let one soldier become a child again
and with his bayonet write the words
of buddha in the sand

when tank fires burn the lips of wind
and earth tosses in sleep
let one soldier become a child again
and making of his tank a plough
furrow the land for new seed

when the world bleeds with the voice of my lai
and hiroshima falls upon the cheeks
let one soldier become a child again
and pitching his bullets into the sky
watch them wheel like birds that cause no pain

JOHN AGARD

Barlinnie*: The World

(slowly, in a Glasgow accent)

It's when ye start tae reach fer the stars,
Ye first find out ye're behind these bars.

Ye can't believe ye're caught in a cage,
An ye exhaust yerself in horrible rage.

Ye think: "What A need's more knowledge, eh?"
An ye read a' ye can get hud o' on bar-ology.

But the more ye read o bars an chains
Hammers disaster intae yer brains.

An then its plans an bombs an guns:
"If A can't be a man, A'll be like the Huns."

But it doesnae work and ye begin tae sink,
An ye get so low ye begin tae think:

"A'll ask ma mates tae gie me a hand,"
But they're a' playin games in the compound sand,

An watchin tellie an studyin' form.
"Aw c'mon," ye say, "this is not for what we wuz born."

"What stars, what bars, what's up wi' you?
Whaddiye mean there's somethin tae do?"

An they begin to ignore ye an tap their heids:
"He's queer, him; when ye cut 'im, he bleeds."

O.K. That's it. Screw them – rejection.
Put me down for the dejection section.

Maybe they're right tae sit on their asses,
Maybe the stars are just hot gasses.

"It'll a' be the same in a hundred years,"
Someone shouts as he wades through yer tears.

But ye don't gie a fuck, ye've closed yer folder;
An then ye feel this hand on yer shoulder,

An ye shake it off, an let out a curse:
Lea' me alone, ye're just makin it worse."

But he doesnae go, he sits down instead,
An ye hear these words comin intae yer head.

"C'mon, pal, Gie us a break. If you sulk alone,
That just leaves me out here on ma own."

An for a moment ye're stuck, an tempted by night,
But ye've got tae look round, cos ye know he's right;

An when ye do, tae yer great surprise,
The Stars, the furthest stars, are in his eyes.

* Barlinnie is a prison in Glasgow.

ALAN JACKSON

Her Gift To Me

Before this, I was sucking
at death's breast, gasping for more
whey as bitter as soot. I
gagged on spoonfuls of ash.

I paused, I gathered my skirts, raced upwards
dropping the world. I hung on and flew. To the dream city
I always believed in: true, though invisible
like the kingdom of God.

Down again. Crushed. I crawled the sidewalk grids
the repeated intersection strobe. Giants played Monopoly:
skyscrapers for dice, the green dollar bills of Central Park.
The food was fake, chic plastic suppers for dolls.

Everybody wanted so much, including me.
The rich ate the poor, then shat them into the subways
and the junkies' eyes were derelict lots, reflecting
the needles of syringe buildings poking at a lost skin.

Rescue. Down West Eleventh Street
a woman sat on her front
steps combing a cat. When she looked
at me I saw her black tadpole eyes.

She waved her fist, and the houses suddenly stopped.
She opened her palm and breathed
and the sky sprang up and out
uncreased, enormous, wholly blue. Her miracle.

The wind uncorked my mouth
and the Hudson river poured in.
I abandoned myself like a coat
and the river flowed through me.

We walked on the water, the salty wooden tongue
of the rotting pier, in a swarm of light.
She hugged herself like a secret sea:
'Once, here, we saw an albatross.'

In the cab cantering up Fifth Avenue, waltzing
from lane to lane with yellow grace
God sat beside me on the leatherette seat
and the driver sang to the wheel: 'go, baby, go.'

Along the New Jersey turnpike I rocked, straphanging
with both hands in the glass bus.
Oil refineries and trees streamed through my eyes and skin.
The hill of God inside and out. The end of me.

MICHÈLE ROBERTS

Holomovement

for Su

(The apple-seed, a memory of the whole tree)
Round-headed sperm in wet millions, manifest.

The ovum excites. At fertilisation
The tissue walls of the enormous cell electrify,

Mitochondria fizzing with the passage of oxygen
And protein mosaics reformulating

As nucleic acids cluster, jiggling,
And a calcium holocaust erupts–

A white, granular cloudburst, the cell,
Weather-dense, storms into repeated division.

The embryo grows, in-pouring skin
That evolves as delicate, shiny gut;

The middle tissue forms the first muscle, as thin
As cellophane, that includes the rippling, transparent heart;

And, for a while, there are primitive gills gently
Feathering with the rhythms of the thin brine of the womb.

Womb sac, an open eye and ear to light and sound,
To changing wavelength, to the clear pulse

Of the mother's blood through the thin umbilicus,
And the deep, regular echo of her heartbeat.

The embryo grows negentropically,
Energy into matter, wave and particle manifest.

The newborn unfolds to air encased in a
Buttery velnix and a hardening tracery of blood–

A memory-membrane beneath which his skin
Enfolds to tiny, shimmering gut villi, fingers

Across which shining food slips, protein polishing protein,
The variously-coloured milk of the mother sucked deep,

Drawn inside, like an arcing, sustenant rainbow.
The mother's milk is coloured by her whole current.

The baby shits from its bright gut as it is born.
Mingling his with the mother's blood such that

Sustenance and excrement are mirrored as equally-valued aspects
Of the same movement, common inspiratrix.

The rotating head guides the body at birth, the child
Hauling behind him the iridescent placenta on belly-string.

The second birth—a resurrected body,
A second coming; expelled yolk, oily and nutritious.

The mother's interior light made plain, a holomovement,
Unfoldment complete as the navel is tied, then

Boy rolls off the glistening
Belly of the mother, refracting light,

Inspired by gravity; baby and mother breathing in rounds,
Light manifesting on each round of breath.

The apple-seed, a memory of the whole tree.

ALAN BLEAKLEY

The Crossing Over

Everyone gone, but the party lamps
still suffuse the hot night
waxen as pears, oil-smelling,
ensnaring moths. A lone
high-heeled shoe
is beginning to shine in the grass.

Delivering yourself you offer
nothing more solid
than a series of images, grainy
and formless as water.
Your footsoles are luminous, your bones
glow in their transparent envelope.
I thought I dreamed you as you came
pushing back the muscle of my ocean.

You bring something costly
as fruit out of season –
the instinct of a night plane
searching for its aerodrome.

I feel your first
systolic touch
on entering the pull of gravity.

PIPPA LITTLE

Seal

As often, behind the ribs, like a seal
Caught in an undertow, the heart dips,
Lurches in broken seas, in turmoil.

But you, real seal in the cove, you roll
In seas twice the height of yourself,
Your polished back, more grey than sky

Curves with the rondure of sea,
And dives – to a calm palace of glass
To watch the anger from under?

An absence where you were. No creature
Is anywhere so at home as you are ...
From black rocks your armour

Is only soft roundness, shining. Dark-helmeted bather,
Not eating, enjoying, again you are there,
A static snout, in turmoil: 'See

I am round as the waves and the world, the
Warmth in cold, anywhere
Else I bark and slither. Master
Of sea – no – the sea my twin.
Sea is the love I am in.'

P.J. KAVANAGH

Second Look At A Cockroach

I can say this:
That I have seen
You are not black
But burnished like a deep
Rich jewel,
Light anointing the smooth armoury
Of your back.
And your feet
Scuttle to their mission
In precise synchronisation.
You go straight to your purpose.
You will even die
With each foot perfectly placed
On your own path,
And in the singleness of being
No one but yourself.

HEATHER KIRK

Things

What I'll miss most when I'm dead is
things that the light shines on.
If there aren't wet leaves in Heaven
then almost I don't want to go there.
If there isn't the possibility
of silly particulars
like library cards on a table
then I almost don't want to go there.
Library cards – because here some happen to be.
I am a small Englishman in an Infinite Universe
looking at library cards. That's funny.
In fact it frightens me.

•

I am in my room, surrounded by the things
which have somehow clung to my existence:
a picture of squirrels, a desk with inkstains
(it was my grandfather's before me),
a Buddha and a jar of Nivea,
a pottery lion lying among rosepetals.
These are my things. They comfort
and encumber me.

But Buddha, what about you?
Your sides are so sheer.
You gave all your riches away.
And can you still hold
on to yourself as a person?

Did Christ give up his things too?
He had a seamless garment.
The other things came when he needed them,
a coin in a fishes' mouth,
ointment for his feet,
a crown of thorns.
Well, he didn't despise things.
He ate bread readily.
He loved the boats of his disciples.

•

And it's not just things that we love,
but one thing next to another –
this African violet beside the tuning fork,
this pen in my hand
as the rain outside falls among Quinces.
These things have happened before;
but when I happen to be there
and notice the shape of the space between them
then a new thing arises in the Universe.
This was unplanned.
This event without Karma.

Angels, though infinitely greater than us,
know nothing of this.
But Christ knows it.
He came for that purpose –
to write on a particular ground
with his little finger.

•

The Gods have enough of Immortality
and need things.
They need cuckoos in a damson tree,
they need rhubarb flapping beside a gate.
Their paternoster is an honest man
who can hammer a nail straight.

PAUL MATTHEWS

Ordinary Things, Once Discovered Never Forgotten

The shew-stone that is a black mirror
Parceled in the tight earth like a black pearl
For millenia, surfacing shiny with its history:
A lump of ordinary coal, unpacking its light to the scryer
Who in his gazing reaps the harvest
Held by the crushed bones of trees, his eyes
Sipping the jet woodgrain that lay sour for years.

The nipple-topped fungus whose musty alkaloids
Are gnomic, burrowing in the brain stem
To spike the regular rhythms of the senses
With unnatural visions, caricaturing those normally
Suspended in the crack where day meets night,
Where space and sound unnerve the chemicals of mind
Making moonshine in the oldest established still,

A heady sourmash that restores sight to the purblind,
Distilled by Eve in the red dirt of Africa's savannah.

ALAN BLEAKLEY

from Tantris

9

we did not recognise
and so we are here
earth-logged in the bardo of words
colour taste touch sound gesture
born and lost each moment

we're among the last of the roselight
silking stubble-fields in Kent

we're in a chatter of aluminium and china
at closing time in a red-faced cafe
in Hull Liverpool Crewe Doncaster

in a dyke bottom, or at the edge of a field
waiting for the pure moment
as the dusk-glint of a fly's wing
vanishes among dusty lofts of nettles

we're on Earth in a furious century
as the voice announces a programme of dance-music
as the performing elephant is led off
without applause
as the rehearsal stops in mid-phrase
as paper cups are knocked over in the gloom
the scene fades quickly to black
and a single unspoken shape
sails around the world
at the speed of fear
glazing eyes
inward

or we're on Earth in a nameless country
in April,
turning and turning
rounding a corner
finding a gate
seeing suddenly the fields
holding up their filmy hands
the question nobody had dared to ask
the latch nobody had dared to try
the tide turning
licking itself clean
dreaming itself free again
and iris and anemone
as they were in the beginning
not reproving but returning
light with light
not caring but caressing and recrossing space
for our wealth and welfare,
our turning about in the deepest seat –
one giant leap for a man,
one small step for mankind

10

Early I rose in the blue morning

> *with beauty before me*

Nor could I guess what kind of thing
I long'd for

but my senses discovered

> *comfrey coltsfoot camomile cinquefoil daisy*

Earth with me
Fire over me

> *blue heart of rain, white heart of rain*

when we clap our hands we know
that there are many of us

and you O ancient flame;
may you hover above my breast as I sleep
help me to cross the bardo's dangerous pathway

> *in old age, wandering on a trail of beauty*
> *living again, may I walk*

Blasket   Cape Wrath   Lizard   Northey

on Papago mountains
the dying stag
looks at me with my love's eyes

> He   Ya   Ha   Ya   Hei!

                              wandering

use everything well

in her house of clouds
in cloud banners, liquid necklaces
in water, mist, somewhere

> *in beauty*
> *it's finished*

STEPHEN PARR

from Global Force

VII

Earth Movers

Earth movers.
Earth tremours.
Earth avalanches.
Casting away
whole hillsides.
Grassy knolls
taking the leap
– to save themselves.

The mud
    ooze
settles.

The whole earth
become a burial place
– for itself.

Turf unto turf.
Fold unto fold.

Earth exposed
– unceremoniously.
The darkest side
   of the Globe
unsealed.

Earth
– burial chamber –
to a million
… forms of life.

Earth
… incubator.
Where cavarns abound.
The darkest of darkness
– eggs, rivulets, eyes
– – and nothing dies.

X

Primal Tasks

To transform.
That is the Work of Art.

The darkest, blackest
   days have come.
Great are the voices
   there to meet them.

New challenges.
New directions.
New, and fresh ideas
   are wanting.

The Courage. The Strength.
To find a way
... from within.

From within
there is something
                to create
                to fire
                to transform
                ... to inspire.

TAGGART DEIKE

Paradise: A Regain – ?

Puncture
Penetrate
Revive, release
Resurrect this hour in your own names
   from the lines of your faces

Grasp the word
    by its roots
Weed out its meanings from their hallowed–
                              corruptive places

Transform your sheets
    of news
Of streets, centuries-crazy-paved:
a muddle-huddle grown grim-faced, now mass-produced.
Still a mould for contradictions: diseased, discrete
                            in their deprivations.

Fixed
spectacles of misery
face the sun
demystified, you people
– once a wonder of this world –

Turn your heads
again with ease, repossess your time
                noise, acts of love
                    yourselves luminous
                        spaces

                                          ANNA TAYLOR

The Hugging Child

'Except ye become as little children...'

Where is the hugging child
in most adults
I should like to know?

Extinct
Murdered

Or merely waiting to come alive?

                                          JOHN HORDER

Gnome-flash

Gnomenreichen
Gnomenreichen
Clinking hammer
Brittle earth

Fascinating
Sparkling crystal
Shining eyes
Sudden mirth

O how thick
The humans are
Thick thick thinking
O how dense

Dreaming dimwits
We are quickwits
Swiftly flitting
Through the flints

Flowing through
The ferrous ores
Inside outside
Out of doors

But the sturdy roots
Are waiting
Us to bring their
Exaltation!

CHARLES LAWRIE

When Children and Poets

You green hill perched under the Edge
Where a word plucked from the wind
Would do for a toy
The brook ran away for our feet
Acorns were suddenly pipes

    an oak tree stencilled
   our day-dreams on winter-
  nights

We took to the air
A cluster of angels with fun on their minds
As faint tricks of light scribbled you notes
Round the goat and plough.
Still write you signs for the times;
Tremble across roof-tops: are clouds

ANNA TAYLOR

First Visit To Glastonbury Tor

It was evening when I first saw her,
rising beyond the pastureland,
in the fine rain, the clover smells,
she held me fast before her
in a great keeping still.

She's deceptive from a distance,
you'd never realize how steep
those thistle succulent sides,

stamp hard on her broad back beneath me –
she ups and throws me –
in the wind fights me in a love fight –
unlocks all my bones –
all that holds them in my shape
in this wild breath on me,

look down,
the flat fields darken with cloud pass.

No solemn eyed musings up here
thank you very much.
A good laugh she wants –
bellies and boots and rough and tumble,

I am a vast cave
containing a carnival.

Grounded, four flights up in London
I laugh out loud when I remember
how she made me show off for her,
when I think of the mystical awakening
I'd been hoping for,
she turned me head over heels
into a child again.

                                                         ANNEMARIE COOPER

Joyful We Dance On The Tyrant Perfection

We dance on
virgin lawns
stamp patterned
footprints on
untroubled whiteness
as we each
in our need for
confirmation
proclaim to the
unnamed observer
our sin
like children
lost in the
ego's cry for
attention
we brand our
ragged confessions
on this
unravished snow
offering its
perfection on
the altar of
our mortality
and hear
God's laughter
on the wind.

                                                       BARBARA S. COLE

Touch

The sun in affirmation
Moves through leaf, through glass,
In bedroom silence lifts
Colour from a sleeping couple.

They touch, they rise,
They carry the touch outwards
Into dressing children,
Into baking bread,
Into painting a chair,

All day through city contact,
All usurious dealings.

The touch passes into walls and vehicles,
Shock-absorbers, telephones.
It becomes the song of the moment,
Gives itself fully
To fade and fray in calm irrelevant beauty.

It evaporates in the moisture
Of eight million pairs of hands
And enters the clouds above the city
To move across the earth
Of deserts and drought places,
The consequence of tenderness,
To bring the soul of matter to the surface,
Hold the world that holds us,
To sometimes fall as rain.

BERNARD SAINT

The Cross In The Milk

milk heats
in the saucepan.

bubbling around
the edges.

before boiling
over,

bubbles push the
skin inwards

making it a
diamond, then a

cross.

an everyday
vision
in my kitchen

BILL LEWIS

Stockwell Good Friday

Stanley sniffs the dusty incense, gazes
on veiled woodwork, hears the wavering plainsong
and decides: – whatever country parishes
might make of primroses and lambs, it's wrong

to think this is some vegetation myth
we celebrate; these people, knelt before a cross
following an old routine, each one must need
some real link to overcoming pain and loss.

Brick hot, the streets outside; late April sun
shines on cracked plasterwork and plastic bags.
Those who have not escaped from town already
are dressed up to kill, in all their glad rags,

and now cruise the streets. Music spills out
of every open window. Back in the year
of the disturbances, it was straightforward,
Stanley thought: the cross, a weapon against fear,

to carry through the ravaged streets, defiant
of the warnings of the police; that seemed
to touch a core. But could the langour
of this burnt-out afternoon now be redeemed?

With just ten minutes of the liturgy to run
there was a message for the owner of his car,
calling him out. The back had just been rammed in
by some joker with a beat-up Jaguar,

unregistered and uninsured, who'd raced away
leaving the tail-lights shattered on the floor,
the near wing buckled in, the bumper bent,
the catch jammed solid on the nearside door.

So Stanley's day concluded with the grieving
over broken bodywork, mopping spilt oil with rags,
binding up torn electrics, trying to dress
gashed panelwork with tape and plastic bags.

And when he finally closed up the garage door,
it was in anger, much more than in sorrow;
he know there'd be no miracle, the metal
wouldn't heal itself when he came back tomorrow.

It made no sense to talk about forgiving:
he wouldn't want a prosecution to be waived.
The damage had been done; what mattered now
was could the Easter holiday be saved?

TONY LUCAS

Beyond All Other

Beyond all other
fear
that we will be unloved
lost faded in our lives without
the golden mark of youth on our cuff,
there is the knowing that always
we are part.

Beyond all other
hope
love is
being wide open to another, total
vulnerability. An exchange of selves.

Beyond all other
desire
there is the idea of eternity
we listen for its ghosts
finding habit, pattern.

Beyond all other
love
there is this extension of self
moving out against the inertia
the laziness we call work.
Moving out in the face of all fears
courage.
Moving out towards desire
value creates love.
Love then is a form of work
of courage.

"What massive stones. What magnificent buildings."

ELAINE RANDELL

* * * * *

CODA

The Witches Farmed Omens

When quicksand
stirs an egg
under a rainbow
words brewed
in a drunken river
push bruised cloth
underground
and timed fruit
explodes
seams of polarity
into love.

LINDA KING

THE PITY OF THE WORLD
IS ONLY THE SHADOW OF TRUTH.

LEMN SISSAY

The Angel And The Star

In the deep of midnight blue
the stars are beckoning.
If you travel that way
you will see light so clear and pure
it will become lambent
and enfold you in its substance.

That is oneness.

LIZZIE SPRING

Benediction

Thanks to the ear
that someone may hear

Thanks to seeing
that someone may see

Thanks to feeling
that someone may feel

Thanks to touch
that one may be touched

Thanks to flowering of white moon
and spreading shawl of black night
holding villages and cities together

                                            JAMES BERRY

"Tell them how easy love is"

How the light mist comes up and across
the marsh in late afternoon
how the big trees are so big.
If I was a man the love of a good woman
would keep me safe and wear me out.
Tiny flowers in the wood tonight
I picked a few and brought them home.
Crow and sheep share the same water trough
Just the way the light rises
up drawing together the day and the voices
of the people warm in their homes.
O tell them how easy love is.

                                      ELAINE RANDELL

Let The Centre Hold

When the new octave begins
There is a power in the wind,
And the race is on to be first at the waking;
And neither party knows the names
Of this game to end all games,
And somewhere deep you know the earth is shaking:
Then let the centre hold, only let the centre hold.

When there are wings in every cloud
And I shout your name aloud,
And I know that soon there'll be an end to waiting;
When you find you are the key
To this nameless mystery,
And you begin to see the doorway I am making:
Then let the centre hold, only let the centre hold.

When the brilliance of your star
Shows me just how close you are,
Though you may have been a million light years falling;
And it may blow the world apart
When you land inside my heart,
Though the cherry blooms and all the birds are calling:
Then let the centre hold, oh please let the centre hold.

I am standing quite alone
Before a secret standing stone,
And there are faces in the mist banks of the morning;
And the last fears are all shed
From the caverns of the dead,
And along light rays of dawn I see you coming:
Then let the centre hold, oh please let the centre hold.
Let the centre hold.
Let the centre hold.

Jehanne Mehta

AFTERWORD

Poetry has largely dropped out of our culture. The majority of people read it rarely. It no longer really matters. Why is this?

For the last three centuries we have cultivated the masculine, analytical intellect, which we are told operates from the left hemisphere of the brain. Its faculty is to separate and isolate and it is therefore used to control nature. So we have developed the onlooker consciousness and use intellect to get things and satisfy desires. Thus the sensitive feminine faculties of the right hemisphere have largely atrophied and gone dormant for lack of use. And these springs of the Imagination are the source and channel for poetry. Through this magic casement we can apprehend the vast living Oneness of the Universe. The true faculty of Imagination opens the vision of the Whole of which we are each integrally part. The poet is one through whom the life of nature flows and crystallizes into expression. Thus we can learn to take a poem and work into it and impregnate our understanding with it, knowing that here is a virgin spring bubbling out of the ocean of Life. Then we are overcoming the onlooker consciousness and merging with the life-source.

In our generation, a breakthrough is taking place into holistic vision, a turn-about in the centre of our consciousness enabling us to know by direct experience that the Universe is Mind, Planet Earth a living creature, and Nature a work of art and divine design, of which humanity is the crown in consciousness.

Thus a poem can be *used* by the reader to awaken and develop a higher consciousness. This is something much more than academic (left-hemisphere) study of the work. It is a creative deed in which we activate these dormant faculties.

It is the restoring of our true humanity as the "Vast being of the Imagination" (in Blake's phrase). We may see that the use of poetry is of supreme significance in the widening of consciousness. We can all work at this, and the poets of our time who can really tap the springs within themselves are doing a major service to awakening humanity.

Thus this anthology: *Transformation – the poetry of spiritual consciousness,* represents a trend of vital significance. May it be *read* and thus contribute to the spiritual adventure and awakening of our time.

George Trevelyan

ACKNOWLEDGEMENTS

For permission to reprint copyright material, the publisher gratefully acknowledges the following:

Open Township for Alan Jackson's "West Man", "The Way Is Clear", "The Powers", and "Barlinnie: The World" (from *Heart Of The Sun*); Nadder/Element Books for Carolyn Askar's "Human Mayflies" (from *Spirit Of Fire*); *The Green Book* for William Oxley's "Blind Angel"; Hangman Books for Bill Lewis' "Archbishop Romero" and "The Cross In The Milk" (from *Communion*); Wynstones Press for Charles Lawrie's "TWA In Flight" (from *Songs For The New Man*) and "The Second Coming Over Lindisfarne" (from *The Second Coming Over Lindisfarne*); Kavi-Lok for Shruti Pankaj's "The King" and "Behind The Cross" (from *Beyond The Horizon*); Pluto Press for John Agard's "Beat It Out" and "For All Who Fell In Wars Within And Without The Heart Of Man" (from *Mangoes & Bullets*); Methuen for Michèle Roberts' "The Sibyl's Song" and "Her Gift To Me" (from *The Mirror Of The Mother*); Outposts Publications for Lanny Kennish's "Incarnation" (from *Mid-Day*); The Diamond Press for Lizzie Spring's "In The Dark", "The Lioness" and "The Angel And The Star" (from *First Things*); *Writing Women* for Moniza Alvi's "Hill"; The Diamond Press for Geoffrey Godbert's "The Poetry Of Birth" (from *Journey To The Edge Of Light*); Duckworth for Gladys Mary Cole's "Water Image" and "The Sounding Circle" (from *Leafburners*); Turret Books for Harry Fainlight's "For The First Bird At Dawn", "Excabbala" and "Wolstonbury" (from *Selected Poems*); Dollar Of Soul Audio for Owen Davis', "Ending With A Line of Bronk's", "Arriving Late At The End of Time" (from the cassette tape *Into Another World*, with Pool Of Sound & Frank Perry); Wynstones Press for Lanny Kennish's "Anniversary" (from *The Brook Runs*); Phoenix Press for John Moat's *from* Skeleton Key (*Skeleton Key*); Oxford University Press for James Berry's "Reconsidering", "Rastaman" and "Benediction" (from *Chain Of Days*); Savacou (Jamaica) for A.L. Hendriks' "D'Ou Venons Nous?" (from *The Islanders And Other Poems*); *Resurgence* for William Oxley's "Into The Blaze Of Day"; Chatto & Windus for P.J. Kavanagh's "Air" and "Seal" (from *Selected Poems*); The Diamond Press for Jay Ramsay's "New Age" (from *Divinations*); Virago for Stef Pixner's "Morning" (from *Sawdust And White Spirit*); Pig Press for Elaine Randell's "On Sighting The First Bluebell", "Beyond All Other" and "Tell them how easy love is" (from *Beyond All Other*); *folded sheets* (Open Township) for Paul Matthews' "Where Beauty Lies"; Routledge & Kegan Paul for Peter Redgrove's "The Party In The Woods" (from *The Man Named East*); Oxford University Press for Penelope Shuttle's "Chrysalis" (from *The Lion Came From Rio*); Pennyfields Press for Stephen Parr's *from* Tantris (*Tantris*); Purple Heather for Anna Taylor's "Paradise: A Regain – ?" (*Cut Some Cords*); Link Up for Jehanne Mehta's "Let The Centre Hold".

BRIEF NOTES ON CONTRIBUTORS

Alan Jackson tells his own story best in *Heart Of The Sun* (Open Township): and it is a remarkable one. His most recent book is *Light Hearts* (Sel de Mer Press). "The burning edge/of liberty/is action against oneself". He lives in Edinburgh. **Barbara S. Cole** also works as a Psychosynthesis counsellor, and names the poet in her "Barbara Sky". She lives in Lewes, East Sussex. **Bernard Saint** also works as therapist, and performs work with jazz guitar and quartet. His *Testament Of The Compass* (Burns & Oates) is still available, and double cassette *Welcome Back to the Studio* released this year on Lyrenote. He lives in Bristol. **Carolyn Askar** is a drama and poetry lecturer and actress, and a member of the Angels Of Fire collective. Her main interest lies in the therapeutic value of creative expression, and the body/mind/spirit connections. Her most recent publication is *A Unique Curve* (Priapus Press). She lives in Elstree, Hertfordshire. **William Oxley** is a poet and philosopher, and reviews editor of *Acumen* (ed. Patricia Oxley). He believes that all important truth is revealed, therefore poetry must be a combination of inspiration and craftsmanship. His major work *A Map Of Time* (University of Salzburg) is available. He lives in Higher Furzenham, South Devon. **Stephen Parr** has also worked for the BBC, in graphic design, and arts administration (Bija). His preface to *Tantris* (Pennyfields Press) is a useful introduction. "Poetry... is an act of faith in the reality of forces within us which may perhaps ultimately work to free us from the ocean of conflicts that is our inheritance". He lives in Bristol. **Bill Lewis** was a founder member of the Medway Poets (with Billy Childish and others) and is a regular performer of his poems and chants. His *Communion* (Hangman Books) is available. "See comrade marxist/it is a biological fact/we both wear our hearts/on the same side". He lives in Chatham, Kent. **Charles Lawrie** has four collections, the most recent of which is *Cymric Scriptures* (Wynstones Press). He is also the editor of the new journal *Shoreline: for Metamorphosis*, devoted to impulses of Living Art and Science in poetry and prose (unquote). He lives in Penmorfa, North Wales. **Dinah Livingstone** has published ten collections from Katabasis, and her Selected Poems *Saving Grace* is available from Rivelin Grapheme. She is another fiery performer. She lives in London. **James Berry** is a senior spokesman for Caribbean poetry, reflected in his anthology *News for Babylon*

(Chatto & Windus) and his own *Chain Of Days* (OUP). He lives in Brighton. **Shruti Pankaj** first published her *Beyond the Horizon* (Kavi-Lok) at the age of 15. As Lord Brockway remarked: "At 15! I begin to believe in reincarnation". Her most recent work has been with the Peace Bus, which, with pilgrims from many religious nationalities, travelled through Europe visiting Auschwitz, Belsen, Dachau. She also organizes Culture Relief events. She lives in Mitcham, Surrey. **John Agard**, who was born in Guyana, is a well-loved and very special performer and he works as touring lecturer for the Commonwealth Institute. His publications include *Man To Pan, Limbo Dancer In Dark Glasses* and *Mangoes & Bullets,* which is a Selected (Pluto Press). He lives in Lewes, East Sussex. **Michèle Roberts** has published four novels, including *The Wild Girl* (Methuen) and as a feminist has contributed essays to a series of other books which reflect her preoccupation with a redemptive, feminized and embodied spirituality. She lives in London. **Gillian Allnutt** was for four years poetry editor of *City Limits* magazine and was a member of Angels of Fire. Her publications include *Spitting The Pips Out* (Sheba) and *Beginning the Avocado* (Virago). She now lives in Newcastle. **Alan Rycroft** belongs to the Da Free John (Da Love Ananda) community. His work (which includes a play about the 17th C. visionary George Fox) is as yet unpublished. His "Poetry As Sacred Act, or Sacrament Of Heart-Communication" is a brilliant, timeless manifesto that all his poems enlarge on. He lives in London. **Lanny Kennish** was born in New York, has taught English at Wynstones (Steiner) School and is also a bioremedial masseur. Published by Wynstones Press, her books include *The Brook Runs* and *The Bloom On The Stone*. "If love be anything/It is to hold tight to the earth/As it whirls...". She lives in Brookthorpe, Gloucestershire. **Andy Peters** is a performance poet, didgeridoo player, improvising singer and playshop leader, and has done voice work with Chloe Goodchild and Gilles Petit. His *The Ways Of Light And Laughter* (poems and photographs for the New Age) is still available. "I am interested in working with others to remember their spontaneity". He lives in Bristol. **Lizzie Spring** co-founded The Badger Poets, has worked as a cleaning lady, caterer, driver, teacher and jobbing gardener, has studied music, Psychosynthesis, and Alfred Wolfsohn's method of voice work, is a composer (piano), also a painter, and a member of Angels of Fire. Her *First Things* is published by The Diamond

Press (illustrated by herself). She lives in London. **Geoffrey Godbert** is The Diamond Press, and (with Anthony Astbury and Harold Pinter), the Greville Press. As well as their *100 Poems by 100 Poets* (Methuen), his own books include *The Lover Will Dance Incredibly* and his Selected *Journey To The Edge Of Light* (The Diamond Press). He has also worked with Angels of Fire, and in Freelance PR. He lives in London. **Georgina Lock** is an actress and directs and writes for the theatre, with a particular leaning towards musical black comedy. She also collaborates with artists to devise shows around paintings and sculpture through actors' improvisations. She lives in London. **Moniza Alvi** was born in Pakistan, currently teaches at a girls' comprehensive school in South London, and is a member of the Ver Poets. She lives in London. **Timothy Atkins** has written an M.Phil. thesis on John Ashbery, with a special interest in American poetry, astrology and teaching. His *Some Poems* (Tay Press/University of Stirling) is still available. He lives in London. **Paul Matthews** teaches poetry and gymnastics at Emerson College, and gives workshops. His ten or so books and pamphlets include *The Fabulous Names Of Things*. His *The Grammar Of Darkness*, available from Emerson, is an essay and an introduction: his most recent book is *Two Stones, One Bird* with Owen Davis (Smith/Doorstop Press). "O Caroline, I know nothing about the light. But I love what it plays upon". He lives in Forest Row, Sussex. **Harry Fainlight**, brother of Ruth, was found dead in September 1982 by a local farmer outside his remote Welsh cottage; the cause given was bronchial pneumonia. Filmed as part of the *Wholly Communion* Albert Hall reading in 1965, his one published book was *Sussicran* (Narcissus, in mirror writing). Turret Books have published a *Selected Poems*, introduced by Ruth, with memoirs from Allen Ginsberg and Ted Hughes ("Trying to get it right, just how it felt"). His exceptional lyricism is self-evident. **Owen Davis**, born in Kuala Lumpur, has published ten collections, as well as editing *South West Review*, and co-editing (with Jeremy Hilton) Chicken Sigh/Dollar Of Soul Press. Their *1+1* is available from Rivelin Grapheme Press. His cassette tape *Into Another World* with Pool Of Sound & Frank Perry, also available, is a breakthrough in poetry/music collaboration: and he is currently performing the results. He describes his way as "Sufism, set within the boundaries of Islam". He lives in Swanage, Dorset. **Carol Fisher** runs The Open Poetry Conventicle (Putney,

London), and has published one collection, *Mouth Music*, which is designed like an exercise book, and is still available. She lives in London. **Libby Houston** has three collections, including *At The Mercy* (Allison & Busby), has led the Practising Poets workshop, as well as working as an Arvon Foundation tutor, and in conservation. "If you're gold, you can wait". She lives in Bristol. **John Moat**, born in India, has published novels *(Heorot, The Tugen & The Toot, Bartonwood, Mai's Wedding)* as well as poetry. With John Fairfax, he co-founded the Arvon Foundation and Phoenix Press. He is also a trustee of the Yarner Trust (training for organic small holding), and a director of the Environment Research Association, as well as being a regular columnist in *Resurgence* (Didymus). His most recent poetry book is *Welcombe Overtures*. He lives in Hartland, North Devon. **Jo Loncelle**, born in France, worked at the Bibliotheque Nationale, and was involved in left wing and feminist politics. She writes: "soon after my coming to London, I realized I would have to search within myself in my quest for meaning". She then became involved in therapy and astrology, fields in which she now practises as well as writing. She lives in London. **Pippa Little** born in East Africa, has worked in publishing, was an Eric Gregory Award Winner, is a mother, is writing a PhD, has work in various anthologies (Chatto, Salamander, Penguin) and *Edges* (Ampersand Press). "As a socialist and a feminist I am trying to understand inner and outer spaces and how they connect". "Pilgrim Woman" is for her mother. She lives in London. **Anne Born** has four collections, as well as being a regional historian, a translator (from the Scandinavian languages) and an "aspirant novelist". She has been a writer/poet in various residences. "Inspiration: human relationship and the numinous in landscape". She lives in Froude, South Devon. **Rosemary Palmeira,** born in Portugal, is a member of a women's writers' group, and works part-time in Social Work. She has two pamphlets, *A Tuning of Flutes* and *Poems for Birth*, as well as work in magazines and anthologies and a knowledge of contemporary Portuguese poetry. She lives in Kingston-upon-Thames, Surrey. **Sara Jones** has had articles in *Zig Zag, Destiny* and *Exploring the Supernatural*, and has worked, among other things, as a shepherdess. She is currently studying with a view to becoming an archaeologist. Her father is the writer Gonner Jones. She lives in Harpenden, Hertfordshire. **Raymond Tong** worked for the British Council for many years, and is now a freelance writer. As well as education and travel books, he has four collections of poetry, the most recent of which is *Crossing The Border* (Hodder & Stoughton). He lives in Bristol. **Desmond Tarrant** has taught English and American literature at the Universities of Strathclyde, London, Southampton and Maryland (among others), is the author of *James Branch Cabell: The Dream And The Reality* (University of Oklahoma Press), and has a long poem *Sunset Or Sunrise? Or Paradise Found* prefaced by an extended introduction *On Writing A Poem And The Spirit Of Romance*, which he describes as "an attempt to bring Sidney, Milton and Shelley up to date scientifically". "It is time the cycle turned!" He lives in Poole, Dorset. **Snowdon Barnett** is the publisher of Rivelin Grapheme Press, amalgamated from Rivelin Press and Grapheme Publications, and now based in Hungerford where he also runs The Hungerford Bookshop. His publications include *Lines On The Colour Turquoise, Last Entry, Lapis Lazuli* and *Dossiers Secrets*, as well as shorter poems and a long work-in-progress *Now Is As It Pitches*. As a publisher he is committed both to representing a catholic range and expressing values which relate to our changing world in well-produced books that honour their authors and their contents. He lives in Kintbury, Berkshire. **Philip Kane** has one collection *Prayerbeads And Ravenbones* (newly published), "lives with his cat and his addiction to writing" and describes himself as having been described as "the world's first pagan Trotskyist ninja poet". He is also working on The Tarot. He lives in Chatham, Kent. **Les Tate** teaches part-time in a South London comprehensive, cares for two children, and writes poetry and prose fiction. He writes: "Nightmare" is based on James Hillman's *Pan And The Nightmare*. I've been using post-Jungian writers and anthropologists, like Edward Whitmont, Hillman and Eliade to study Shamanism and the lost Dionysos/Pan tradition. I'm interested in integrating this heritage into a more wholistic, less "closed" and repressive version of masculinity". He lives in London. **Linda King** has worked as a black freelance anti-racist, setting up her own anti-racist staff development consultancy (Linda King & Associates), has written her own autobiography *Punch Drunk*, published in anthologies (Sheba, Virago), exhibited in conjunction with visual artists, leads workshops for disabled adults, and performs her poetry. She lives in London. **A.L. Hendriks**, born in Jamaica, had a long career in broadcasting and was chairman of the Arts

Council of Jamaica. His publications include *In This Mountain, These Green Islands, Muet, Madonna Of The Unknown Nation,, The Naked Ghost, The Islanders,* and most recently *To Speak Simply* (Hippopotamus Press): a Selected, and *Check* (with Alan Harris, a talented, forthright, and neglected poet who died last year). He lives in Toddington, Bedfordshire. **Gladys Mary Coles** works as a tutor in Creative Writing at the University of Liverpool, is the author of the standard biography of Mary Webb, *The Flower Of Light* (Duckworth), and the editor and designer of Headland Publications. Her Selected, *Leafburners* (Duckworth) brings poems together from six previous collections. She lives in West Kirby, Merseyside and North Wales. **Andrea Clough** is training to be a counsellor at the Institute of Psychosynthesis, having been an English Literature teacher (specializing in Mediaeval Studies) at London University. Her work, largely unpublished, is beginning to gain the recognition it deserves. She is moving to Suffolk. **Sarah Peel** has also been training in psychotherapy, as well as co-ordinating Password Books, which replaced Southern Distribution as the only outlet for poetry not published and promoted by "major" houses. She now lives in Glasgow. **Alan Bleakley** is a senior lecturer in Psychology at Cornwall College with a particular interest in the Archetypal. Gateway Books have published his *Fruits Of The Moon Tree* (prefaced by Peter Redgrove) and *Earth's Embrace:* both detailing spiritual aspects of the psychological and psychophysical out of which his poetry emerges. He lives in Newmill, Cornwall. **P.J. Kavanagh** works part-time for *The Spectator.* His most recent book is his Selected, *Presences* (Chatto & Windus). He lives in Gloucestershire. **Hilary Norman** runs Open Township with Michael Haslam, and works in the community with mentally handicapped people. "Doubt Not That We Shall Found The City" came to her as a clairaudient experience. She writes: "The reception of these words was preceded by what may best be described as a spiritual experience. Not only spiritual, but earthed by visible remains. Alone in a Scottish glade, two summers ago, I became aware of an uncomfortable, and unaccountable, sense of suffocation. Accustomed to the often difficult results of having an empathic nature, I searched for a cause and found mounds, covered with moss and trefoil. I began to peel back this layer and only stopped when I felt myself again. A number of stones had lain beneath. Two were especially beautiful. One a fallen standing stone, its surface rippled with grey, cream and pale terra-cotta. Nearby, a large crystal in the shape of an egg. Sat beside the latter, I heard a single note that seemed a part of it. I call it the Singing Stone. And its song was of a deep and ageless place where all endeavour is reconciled. Once raised, much later, the standing stone could be seen clearly. The shallow, surface ripples formed a face, indiscernible at close quarters. An expression that blends the bleakness of the Easter Island statues with the calmness of certain Buddhas. And a few days later on a train to Perth, surrounded by Scottish boy cubs with packets of crisps, a voice began to speak to me". She lives in Hebden Bridge, West Yorkshire. **David Stuart Ryan** runs Kozmik Press, has published a travel book on India, and co-ordinates The Troubadour Coffee House readings (Earls Court, London), in the basement. His *Love Poems From Love Worlds* is still available. He lives in London. **Kathleen Raine** (who is 80 this year) is a Blake scholar and editor of the journal *Temenos*, a review devoted to the arts of the imagination. Her Collected Poems is published by George Allen & Unwin. Author of *Defending Ancient Springs*, her most recent collections are *The Presence* and *Selected Poems* (all Golgonooza Press). She writes: "Bernard Blackstone was a distinguished professor of English in Athens and elsewhere in the Near East, author of books on Blake *(English Blake)*, Keats *(The Consecrated Urn)* and other themes dealing with the Romantic poets *(The Lost Traveller)*. He died of cancer in the Marsden Hospital, but a few days before his death experienced a vision of a transition to another world or state, which he was able to write down. This was published in *The Lancet*, attested by three doctors; reprinted in *Light*, the journal of the College of Psychic Studies, and also in the French press. The author of the poem had known him and was much moved by his testimony". She lives in London. **Michael Horovitz** encapsulated a generation in his radical anthology *Children Of Albion* (Penguin), editing *New Departures,* and organising his energetic Poetry Olympics events. More recently: his *Grandchildren Of Albion*, finely articulated blasts of anti-establishment criticism as ever with the spirit of Blake behind him, and his own rural rhapsody *Midsummer Morning Jog Log* (Five Seasons Press, illustrated by Peter Blake). He lives in London and near Bisley, Gloucestershire. **Stef Pixner** has worked in a wide range of occupations from gardener to polytechnic lecturer. Her *Sawdust And White Spirit* is published by Virago. She lives in London. **Elaine**

Randell has published various collections including *Songs For The Sleepless,* and most recently *Beyond All Other* (Pig Press). As Lee Harwood has written: "A writer of our frailties and beauties, of our continual dependence and influence on one another, of 'the compulsion of love' in all its forms". She lives in Bethersden, Kent. **Sara Boyes** has worked in community theatre as an actress/writer, and has regularly contributed poetry to magazines and journals, as well as performing her own work. Married with a child, she also now teaches creative writing. She lives in London. **Peter Redgrove** describes himself as a "Scientist of the Strange", has published prolifically through Routledge & Kegan Paul, and also written plays and experimental novels. His most recent books are his Selected *The Moon Disposes, In The Hall Of The Saurians* (Secker & Warburg), and *The Black Goddess* (Bloomsbury Press). His *The Mudlark Poems & Grand Buveur* are available from Rivelin Grapheme. He lives in Falmouth, Cornwall. **Penelope Shuttle** has also published novels as well as poetry, the most recent collection of which is *The Lion From Rio* (OUP). She also co-authored (with Peter) *The Wise Wound,* a revolutionary study of the magic and power of menstruation recently reprinted. She also lives in Falmouth. **Barbara Zanditon** describes herself as "American, Jewish, middle-aged, working mother, single parent". She writes: "most of my poetry now is inspired by my child whose innocent questions about the meaning of life make me realize how little I know and how much gets shoved under the carpet". She lives in London. **Heather Kirk** returned to writing poetry recently as a result of a process of psychological and spiritual change. Trained in theatre and in particular dance, she is interested in poetry as an expression of the inner dance of the soul manifesting through the physical and the emotional levels... in her own words. She also teaches, and runs a workshop called "The Inner Dance". She lives in London. **Taggart Deike,** born in Denver, U.S.A., is a director, playwright, Peace Movement campaigner and performance poet, and is a member of Angels of Fire and the Playwright's Co-operative. His plays and performance poems include *The Dream Time, The Indiscretions of Judith, Waiting For Hiroshima* and *Global Force,* which he has performed with New York dancer Frances Becker. He lives in London. **Anna Taylor** has worked as a shop assistant, waitress, barmaid, private teacher, industrial artist, civil servant, wife, teacher, translator, literary hack and artist's model (with

French sculptor Serraz). Her *Fausta* is available from Rivelin Grapheme Press. She lives in Fartown, West Yorkshire. **John Horder**, the "hugging poet" is also a bio-energetic therapist and masseur, storyteller and journalist. His publications include *A Sense of Being* (Chatto & Windus) and *Meher Baba And The Nothingness* (Menard Press). He has been working on rebirthing with Sue Geary and Ross Hanneman. "This, too, will pass" – "Old Sufi/ Meher Baba saying to create detachment from maya/illusion, the principle of ignorance which goes on forever". He lives in London. **Annemarie Cooper** is doing an English degree at Birkbeck College, and at the time of writing was "just about to fight to the death with the DHSS". She lives in London. **May Ivimy** is the organiser of Ver Poets (as May Badman), and was given the Dorothy Tutin Award for services to Poetry. Her most recent collection is *Parting the Leaves* (Headland). She lives in St Albans, Hertfordshire. **Tony Lucas** has worked for the last ten years as an Anglican parish priest in Brixton, and his poems have appeared in various magazines and journals *(Ambit, Outposts, Poetry Review, Tribune, Encounter)*. He is working on a book about poetry and spirituality. He lives in London. **Lemn Sissay** has appeared on "Write On" and "Black On Black", has worked for Commonword (promoting and encouraging Black writers in Greater Manchester) from which he developed "Cultureword". His *Tender Fingers In A Clenched Fist* is available from Bogle L'Ouverture. He lives in Manchester. **Jehanne Mehta** is a singer, songwriter and poet, identified with the Troubadour tradition. Her exceptional ability to raise poetry to the level of music is recorded on three Green Jack tapes, accompanied by her husband Rob on fiddle and mandolin alongside her guitar and piano instrumentation. The tapes, including *Pathway With A Heart* are available, and she has recently completed the recording of a master tape (for record) with Alexander Foulcer at Heart & Soul which includes "Let The Centre Hold". She lives in Stroud, Gloucestershire. **Sir George Trevelyan** read history at Cambridge and taught at Gordonstoun. Retiring from the army, he entered adult education and became Warden of Attingham Park, the Shropshire adult college. It was there he did his pioneering work in the teaching of spiritual knowledge as adult education. Retiring from there, he founded the Wrekin Trust, a charitable foundation which has become a focal point for people committed to the exploration of their spiritual natures and the development of consciousness. His books include *Magic Casements* and *A Vision Of The Aquarian Age* (Coventure). He lives near Badminton, Avon.

The cover drawing is by WILLIAM ARKLE and he says of the drawing:

"The vertical line represents the Masculine Element, the horizontal the Feminine Element and the Circle the Circumference of the Being of Divinity. I have made this circumference a loose one so that it can express expansion and I have drawn the lines of the cross the way I have to express a living truth"

Editor's Note

Warm thanks to the following for their help, information and inspiration towards this anthology:

Carole Bruce, Timothy Atkins, Barbara Cole, Paul Matthews, John Fairfax, Sir George Trevelyan, William Arkle, Gillian Allnutt at *City Limits*, Laura Fish from *Ebony* (BBC2), Philip Vine and Jean Shelley at *Words International*, the current members of Angels Of Fire for all their love and support; and, of course, to all the contributors.

First published in 1988
by Rivelin Grapheme Press
The Annexe, Kennet House, 19 High Street,
Hungerford, Berkshire RG17 0NL

in association with Egerton Williams Studio
28 Phipp Street, London EC1

Copyright © in the poems remains with the Authors 1988

Copyright © in the Introduction remains with Jay Ramsay 1988

Copyright © in the Afterword remains with Sir George Trevelyan 1988

Copyright © in the Selection remains with Rivelin Grapheme Press 1988

Printed in England at the Wembley Press,
15 Loverock Road, Battle Farm Trading Estate, Reading, Berkshire.

Typeset by Roger Booth Associates,
18/20 Dean Street, Newcastle upon Tyne NE1 1PG.

Printed on recycled paper.

British Library Cataloguing in Publication Data

Transformation: the poetry of spiritual consciousness
1. Poetry in English, 1945 –. Anthologies.
2. Ramsay, Jay. 1958 –.
821'.914'08

ISBN 0-947612-28-9 (paper)

All rights reserved. No part of this publication may be reproduced, stored in a retrieval system or transmitted in any form or by any means, electronic, mechanical, photocopying, recording or otherwise without the written permission of Rivelin Grapheme Press.

The drawing on the cover is by William Arkle

The cover design is by Edward Egerton-Williams

Of this edition 26 copies have been lettered A to Z and signed by Sir George Trevelyan and Jay Ramsay.

Rivelin Grapheme Press
In association with
Egerton-Williams Studio